Kerry H. Robinsc
Jude Irwin, BSW,
Tania Ferfolja, M
Editors

CW01712653

From Here to Diversity: The Social Impact of Lesbian and Gay Issues in Education in Australia and New Zealand

From Here to Diversity: The Social Impact of Lesbian and Gay Issues in Education in Australia and New Zealand has been co-published simultaneously as *Journal of Gay & Lesbian Social Services*, Volume 14, Number 2 2002.

Pre-publication REVIEWS, COMMENTARIES, EVALUATIONS . . .

"LONG AWAITED. . . challenges the rigid binaries that are produced and reproduced through schooling. . . . A collection that will do much to keep anti-homophobia work on the educational agenda. REQUIRED READING for educators who must take seriously their responsibility to enhance the quality of school life for sexual minority students."

June Larkin, PhD
Director of Equity Studies
University of Toronto

More pre-publication
REVIEWS, COMMENTARIES, EVALUATIONS . . .

"A LANDMARK CONTRIBUTION to educational theory, policy, and practice. . . . Welcome and long overdue. . . . Abounds with implications for fresh appraisals of teacher education, for enriching school-family connections, for making schools safer for all, for making teaching a fulfilling career option for all minorities, and for ensuring that schools and colleges match their rhetoric about excellence, equity, and relevance with their deeds."

Phillip W. Jones, PhD
Pro-Dean, Faculty of Education
The University of Sydney
Australia

"A GROUNDBREAKING BOOK that, for the first time, brings together current educational research on homophobia and heterosexism from Australia and New Zealand in one volume. . . . DESCRIBES EXCITING NEW RESEARCH that is taking place in a variety of educational settings. . . . Representing a wide range of theoretical perspectives, the research collected in this volume provides an understanding of the ways educational researchers have begun to inquire into the nature of homophobia and heterosexism in education and the different ways we can begin to challenge discrimination on the basis of sexual orientation."

Tara Goldstein
Associate Professor
Ontario Institute for Studies in Education
University of Toronto

"IMPORTANT. . . . AN INVALUABLE CONTRIBUTION to under-researched areas in the fields of education, sociology, social psychology, and gay/lesbian studies. . . . Spans a wide range of educational contexts, from elementary and secondary schools to pre-service teacher training and other university programs. Those whose experiences of homophobic discrimination and harassment are documented include young children with lesbian mothers, adolescents and young adults in the school or university system, and older women and men working in educational settings."

Helen Jefferson Lenskyj, PhD
Professor, Department of Sociology and Equity Studies in Education
University of Toronto

Harrington Park Press

From Here to Diversity: The Social Impact of Lesbian and Gay Issues in Education in Australia and New Zealand

From Here to Diversity: The Social Impact of Lesbian and Gay Issues in Education in Australia and New Zealand has been co-published simultaneously as *Journal of Gay & Lesbian Social Services,* Volume 14, Number 2 2002.

The *Journal of Gay & Lesbian Social Services* Monographic "Separates"

From Here to Diversity: The Social Impact of Lesbian and Gay Issues in Education in Australia and New Zealand, edited by Kerry H. Robinson, PhD, MA, BA, DipEd, Jude Irwin, BSW, MA, and Tania Ferfolja, MA, BEd (Vol. 14, No. 2, 2002). *"Long awaited. . . challenges the rigid binaries that are produced and reproduced through schooling. . . A collection that will do much to keep anti-homophobia work on the educational agenda. Required reading for educators who must take seriously their responsibility to enhance the quality of school life for sexual minority students." (June Larkin, PhD, Director of Equity Studies, University of Toronto)*

Midlife and Aging in Gay America, edited by Douglas C. Kimmel, PhD, and Dawn Lundy Martin, MA (Vol. 13, No. 4, 2001). *"MAGNIFICIENT. This is a topic whose time has finally come. This book fills a gaping hole in the GLBT literature. . . . Each chapter is a gem. With its coverage of elder GLBT's who are vision impaired and HIV positive as well as an important chapter on GLBT retirement planning, it makes the literature human and integrated." (Mark Pope, EdD, Associate Professor of Counseling and Family Therapy, University of Missouri, St. Louis)*

From Hate Crimes to Human Rights: A Tribute to Matthew Shepard, edited by Mary E. Swigonski, PhD, LCSW, Robin S. Mama, PhD, and Kelly Ward, LCSW (Vol. 13, No. 1/2, 2001). *An unsparing look at prejudice and hate crimes against LGBT individuals, in such diverse areas as international law, the child welfare system, minority cultures, and LGBT relationships.*

Working-Class Gay and Bisexual Men, edited by George Alan Appleby, MSW, PhD, (Vol. 12, No. 3/4, 2001). Working-Class Gay and Bisexual Men *is a powergully persuasive work of scholarship with broad-ranging implications. Social workers, policymakers, AIDS activists, and anyone else concerned with the lives of gay and bisexual men will find this informative study as essential tool for designing effective programs.*

Gay Men and Childhood Sexual Trauma: Integrating the Shattered Self, edited by James Cassese, MSW, CSW (Vol. 12, No. 1/2, 2000). *"An excellent, thought-provoking collection of essays. Therapists who work with gay men will be grateful to have such a comprehensive resource for dealing with sexual trauma." (Rik Isensee, LCSW, Author of* Reclaiming Your Life*)*

Midlife Lesbian Relationships: Friends, Lovers, Children, and Parents, edited by Marcy R. Adelman, PhD (Vol. 11, No. 2/3, 2000). *"A careful and sensitive look at the various relationships of [lesbians at midlife] inside and outside of the therapy office. A useful addition to a growing body of literature." (Ellyn Kaschak, PhD, Professor of Psychology, San José State University, California, and Editor of the feminist quarterly journal* Women & Therapy)

Social Services with Transgendered Youth, edited by Gerald P. Mallon, DSW (Vol. 10, No. 3/4, 1999). *"A well-articulated book that provides valuable information about a population that has* *been virtually ignored. . . ." (Carol T. Tully, PhD, Associate Professor, Tulane University, School of Social Work, New Orleans, Louisiana)*

Queer Families, Common Agendas: Gay People, Lesbians, and Family Values, edited by T. Richard Sullivan, PhD (Vol. 10, No. 1, 1999). *Examines the real life experience of those affected by current laws and policies regarding homosexual families.*

Lady Boys, Tom Boys, Rent Boys: Male and Female Homosexualities in Contemporary Thailand, edited by Peter A. Jackson, PhD, and Gerard Sullivan, PhD (Vol. 9, No. 2/3, 1999). *"Brings to life issues and problems of interpreting sexual and gender identities in contemporary Thailand." (Nerida M. Cook, PhD, Lecturer in Sociology, Department of Sociology and Social Work, University of Tasmania, Australia)*

Working with Gay Men and Lesbians in Private Psychotherapy Practice, edited by Christopher J. Alexander, PhD (Vol. 8, No. 4, 1998). *"Rich with information that will prove especially invaluable to therapists planning to or recently having begun to work with lesbian and gay clients in private practice." (Michael Shernoff, MSW, Private Practice, NYC; Adjunct Faculty, Hunter College Graduate School of Social Work)*

Violence and Social Injustice Against Lesbian, Gay and Bisexual People, edited by Lacey M. Sloan, PhD, and Nora S. Gustavsson, PhD (Vol. 8, No. 3, 1998). *"An important and timely book that exposes the multilevel nature of violence against gay, lesbian, bisexual, and transgender people." (Dorothy Van Soest, DSW, Associate Dean, School of Social Work, University of Texas at Austin)*

The HIV-Negative Gay Man: Developing Strategies for Survival and Emotional Well-Being, edited by Steven Ball, MSW, ACSW (Vol. 8, No. 1, 1998). *"Essential reading for anyone working with HIV-negative gay men." (Walt Odets, PhD, Author, In the Shadow of the Epidemic: Being HIV-Negative in the Age of AIDS; Clinical Psychologist, private practice, Berkeley, California)*

School Experiences of Gay and Lesbian Youth: The Invisible Minority, edited by Mary B. Harris, PhD (Vol. 7, No. 4, 1998). *"Our schools are well served when authors such as these have the courage to highlight problems that schools deny and to advocate for students whom schools make invisible." (Gerald Unks, Professor, School of Education, University of North Carolina at Chapel Hill; Editor, The Gay Teen.) Provides schools with helpful suggestions for becoming places that welcome gay and lesbian students and, therefore, better serve the needs of all students.*

Rural Gays and Lesbians: Building on the Strengths of Communities, edited by James Donald Smith, ACSW, LCSW, and Ronald J. Mancoske, BSCW, DSW (Vol. 7, No. 3, 1998). *"This informative and well-written book fills a major gap in the literature and should be widely read." (James Midgley, PhD, Harry and Riva Specht Professor of Public Social Services and Dean, School of Social Welfare, University of California at Berkeley)*

Gay Widowers: Life After the Death of a Partner, edited by Michael Shernoff, MSW, ACSW (Vol. 7, No. 2, 1997). *"This inspiring book is not only for those who have experienced the tragedy of losing a partner-it's for every gay man who loves another." (Michelangelo Signorile, author, Life Outside)*

Gay and Lesbian Professionals in the Closet: Who's In, Who's Out, and Why, edited by Teresa DeCrescenzo, MSW, LCSW (Vol. 6, No. 4, 1997). *"A gripping example of the way the closet cripples us and those we try to serve." (Virginia Uribe, PhD, Founder, Project 10 Outreach to Gay and Lesbian Youth, Los Angeles Unified School District)*

Two Spirit People: American Indian Lesbian Women and Gay Men, edited by Lester B. Brown, PhD (Vol. 6, No. 2, 1997). *"A must read for educators, social workers, and other providers of social and mental health services." (Wynne DuBray, Professor, Division of Social Work, California State University)*

Social Services for Senior Gay Men and Lesbians, edited by Jean K. Quam, PhD, MSW (Vol. 6, No. 1, 1997). *"Provides a valuable overview of social service issues and practice with elder gay men and lesbians." (Outword)*

Men of Color: A Context for Service to Homosexually Active Men, edited by John F. Longres, PhD (Vol. 5, No. 2/3, 1996). *"An excellent book for the 'helping professions.'"* *(Feminist Bookstore News)*

Health Care for Lesbians and Gay Men: Confronting Homophobia and Heterosexism, edited by K. Jean Peterson, DSW (Vol. 5, No. 1, 1996). *"Essential reading for those concerned with the quality of health care services." (Etcetera)*

Sexual Identity on the Job: Issues and Services, edited by Alan L. Ellis, PhD, and Ellen D. B. Riggle, PhD (Vol. 4, No. 4, 1996). *"Reveals a critical need for additional research to address the many questions left unanswered or answered unsatisfactorily by existing research." (Sex Roles: A Journal of Research) "A key resource for addressing sexual identity concerns and issues in your workplace." (Outlines)*

Human Services for Gay People: Clinical and Community Practice, edited by Michael Shernoff, MSW, ACSW (Vol. 4, No. 2, 1996). *"This very practical book on clinical and community practice issues belongs on the shelf of every social worker, counselor, or therapist working with lesbians and gay men." (Gary A. Lloyd, PhD, ACSW, BCD, Professor and Coordinator, Institute for Research and Training in HIV/AIDS Counseling, School of Social Work, Tulane University)*

Violence in Gay and Lesbian Domestic Partnerships, edited by Claire M. Renzetti, PhD, and Charles Harvey Miley, PhD (Vol. 4, No. 1, 1996). *"A comprehensive guidebook for service providers and community and church leaders." (Small Press Magazine)*

Gays and Lesbians in Asia and the Pacific: Social and Human Services, edited by Gerard Sullivan, PhD, and Laurence Wai-Teng Leong, PhD (Vol. 3, No. 3, 1995). *"Insights in this book can provide an understanding of these cultures and provide an opportunity to better understand your own." (The Lavender Lamp)*

Lesbians of Color: Social and Human Services, edited by Hilda Hidalgo, PhD, ACSW (Vol. 3, No. 2, 1995). *"An illuminating and helpful guide for readers who wish to increase their understanding of and sensitivity toward lesbians of color and the challenges they face." (Black Caucus of the ALA Newsletter)*

Lesbian Social Services: Research Issues, edited by Carol T. Tully, PhD, MSW (Vol. 3, No. 1, 1995). *"Dr. Tully challenges us to reexamine theoretical conclusions that relate to lesbians. . . A must read." (The Lavender Lamp)*

HIV Disease: Lesbians, Gays and the Social Services, edited by Gary A. Lloyd, PhD, ACSW, and Mary Ann Kuszelewicz, MSW, ACSW (Vol. 2, No. 3/4, 1995). *"A wonderful guide to working with people with AIDS. A terrific meld of political theory and hands-on advice, it is essential, inspiring reading for anyone fighting the pandemic or assisting those living with it." (Small Press)*

Addiction and Recovery in Gay and Lesbian Persons, edited by Robert J. Kus, PhD, RN (Vol. 2, No. 1, 1995). *"Readers are well-guided through the multifaceted, sometimes confusing, and frequently challenging world of the gay or lesbian drug user." (Drug and Alcohol Review)*

Helping Gay and Lesbian Youth: New Policies, New Programs, New Practice, edited by Teresa DeCrescenzo, MSW, LCSW (Vol. 1, No. 3/4, 1994). *"Insightful and up-to-date, this handbook covers several topics relating to gay and lesbian adolescents . . . It is must reading for social workers, educators, guidance counselors, and policymakers." (Journal of Social Work Education)*

Social Services for Gay and Lesbian Couples, edited by Lawrence A. Kurdek, PhD (Vol. 1, No. 2, 1994). *"Many of the unique issues confronted by gay and lesbian couples are addressed here." (Ambush Magazine)*

From Here to Diversity: The Social Impact of Lesbian and Gay Issues in Education in Australia and New Zealand

Kerry H. Robinson, PhD, MA, BA, DipEd
Jude Irwin, BSW, MA
Tania Ferfolja, MA, BEd
Editors

From Here to Diversity: The Social Impact of Lesbian and Gay Issues in Education in Australia and New Zealand has been co-published simultaneously as *Journal of Gay & Lesbian Social Services*, Volume 14, Number 2 2002.

Harrington Park Press
The Haworth Social Work Practice Press
Imprints of
The Haworth Press, Inc.
New York • London • Oxford

Published by

Harrington Park Press®, 10 Alice Street, Binghamton, NY 13904-1580 USA

Harrington Park Press® is an imprint of The Haworth Press, Inc., 10 Alice Street, Binghamton, NY 13904-1580 USA.

From Here to Diversity: The Social Impact of Lesbian and Gay Issues in Education in Australia and New Zealand has been co-published simultaneously as *Journal of Gay & Lesbian Social Services*, Volume 14, Number 2 2002.

Cover design by Anastasia Litwak

Library of Congress Cataloging-in-Publication Data

From here to diversity : the social impact of lesbian and gay issues in education in Australia and New Zealand / Kerry H. Robinson, Jude Irwin, Tania Ferfolja, editors.

p. cm.

"Co-published simultaneously as Journal of gay & lesbian social services, volume 14, number 2, 2002."

Includes bibliographical references and index.

ISBN 1-56023-550-0 (hard : alk. paper)–ISBN 1-56023-551-9 (pbk : alk. paper)

1. Homosexuality and education–Social aspects–Australia. 2. Homosexuality and education–Social aspects–New Zealand. 3. Gay and lesbian studies. I. Robinson, Kerry H. II. Irwin, Jude. III. Ferfolja, Tania. IV. Journal of gay & lesbian social services.

LC192.6 .F76 2002
370′ .86′64–dc21 2002008454

Indexing, Abstracting & Website/Internet Coverage

This section provides you with a list of major indexing & abstracting services. That is to say, each service began covering this periodical during the year noted in the right column. Most Websites which are listed below have indicated that they will either post, disseminate, compile, archive, cite or alert their own Website users with research-based content from this work. (This list is as current as the copyright date of this publication.)

Abstracting, Website/Indexing Coverage . . . . Year When Coverage Began

- ***caredata CD: the social and community care database <www.scie.org.uk>*** **1994**
- ***CNPIEC Reference Guide: Chinese National Directory of Foreign Periodicals*** **1995**
- ***Contemporary Women's Issues*** **1998**
- ***Criminal Justice Abstracts*** **1997**
- ***Education Research Abstracts (ERA) <www.tandf.co.uk>*** **2001**
- ***ERIC Clearinghouse on Urban Education (ERIC/CUE)*** **1995**
- ***Family Index Database <www.familyscholar.com>*** **2001**
- ***Family Violence & Sexual Assault Bulletin*** **1999**
- ***FINDEX <www.publist.com>*** **1999**
- ***Gay & Lesbian Abstracts <www.nisc.com>*** **1999**
- ***GenderWatch <www.slinfo.com>*** **1999**
- ***HOMODOK/"Relevant" Bibliographic Database*** **1995**

(continued)

- *IBZ International Bibliography of Periodical Literature <www.saur.de>* **1996**
- *IGLSS Abstracts <http://www.iglss.org>* **2000**
- *Index Guide to College Journals (core list compiled by integrating 48 indexes frequently used to support undergraduate programs in small to medium sized libraries)* . . . **1999**
- *Index to Periodical Articles Related to Law* **1994**
- *OCLC Public Affairs Information Service <www.pais.org>* **1995**
- *Psychological Abstracts (PsycINFO) <www.apa.org>* **2001**
- *Referativnyi Zhurnal (Abstracts Journal of the All-Russian Institute of Scientific and Technical Information–in Russian)* **1994**
- *Social Services Abstracts <www.csa.com>* **1999**
- *Social Work Abstracts <www.silverplatter.com/catalog/swab.htm>* **1994**
- *Sociological Abstracts <www.csa.com>* **1994**
- *Studies on Women & Gender Abstracts <www.tandf.co.uk>* **1994**
- *Violence and Abuse Abstracts: A Review of Current Literature on Interpersonal Violence (VAA)* **1995**

Special Bibliographic Notes related to special journal issues (separates) and indexing/abstracting:

- indexing/abstracting services in this list will also cover material in any "separate" that is co-published simultaneously with Haworth's special thematic journal issue or DocuSerial. Indexing/abstracting usually covers material at the article/chapter level.
- monographic co-editions are intended for either non-subscribers or libraries which intend to purchase a second copy for their circulating collections.
- monographic co-editions are reported to all jobbers/wholesalers/approval plans. The source journal is listed as the "series" to assist the prevention of duplicate purchasing in the same manner utilized for books-in-series.
- to facilitate user/access services all indexing/abstracting services are encouraged to utilize the co-indexing entry note indicated at the bottom of the first page of each article/chapter/contribution.
- this is intended to assist a library user of any reference tool (whether print, electronic, online, or CD-ROM) to locate the monographic version if the library has purchased this version but not a subscription to the source journal.
- individual articles/chapters in any Haworth publication are also available through the Haworth Document Delivery Service (HDDS).

From Here to Diversity: The Social Impact of Lesbian and Gay Issues in Education in Australia and New Zealand

CONTENTS

ABOUT THE EDITORS

Kerry H. Robinson, PhD, MA, BA, DipEd, is Senior Lecturer in sociology in the School of Education and Early Childhood Studies at the University of Western Sydney, Australia. She has taught in the area of equity studies with teacher trainees for the past 10 years. Dr. Robinson has written, researched and presented extensively in the area of diversity and difference, particulary in relation to gender and sexuality. Her doctoral thesis investigated sexual harassment in Australian secondary schools, and she has recently completed an investigation into early childhood educators' perceptions, practices, and policies related to diversity, including lesbian and gay sexuality. Her relevant publications include " 'Great Tits, Miss!': The Sexual Harassment of Female Teachers in Secondary Schools" (2000, *Discourse: Studies in the Cultural Politics of Education*), "What Are We Doing This For?: Dealing with Lesbian and Gay Issues in Teacher Education" (2001, *The British Journal of Sociology of Education*) and "Diversity and Difference in Early Childhood Education" (chapter in *The Other Sydney: Communities, Identities, and Inequalities in Western Sydney*, 2000). She is currently a member of the board for the Australian Centre for Lesbian and Gay Research (ACLGR).

Jude Irwin, BSW, MA, is Chair, Department of Social Work, Social Policy, and Sociology at the University of Sydney, Australia. She is a past Director of the Australian Centre for Lesbian and Gay Research (ACLGR) and is currently a board member of that organization. She is an appointed community member of the Council on Violence Against Women in New South Wales, Australia, and is a member of the NSW Child Death Review Team. She has practiced, researched, and written extensively in the areas of violence against women and gay/lesbian issuses. Her publications include three co-edited books: *Community Work or Social Change?; Social Change and Social Welfare Practice;* and *Women and Violence: Working for Change*. She has also published several major research reports, including "*All I Need is My Doona*," *Homelessness Amongst Gay* and *Lesbian Young People*, and *The Pink Ceiling Is Too Low: Workplace Experiences of Lesbians, Gay Men, and Transgender People.*

Tania Ferfolja, MA, BEd, is an experienced school teacher and educational consultant and has worked in the tertiary sector as a lecturer and researcher for the past five years. She is currently undertaking her PhD in sociology at the University of New South Wales, Australia. Her thesis explores the experiences of lesbian teachers in New South Wales high schools and examines the implications of policies and practices that impinge on their lives. She has also been involved in research examining diversity issues in early childhood education with Kerry Robinson. She is particularly interested in teacher education and is a member of a team examining sexuality and pedagogical issues in teacher training courses in universities in New South Wales, Australia, and Ontario, Canada. Her publications include "Australian Lesbian Teachers: A Reflection of Homophobic Harassment in New South Wales Government Schools" (1998, *Gender and Education),* "What Are We Doing This For?: Dealing with Lesbian and Gay Issues in Teacher Education" (2001, *The British Journal of Sociology of Education*), and "Women Live Longer!: The Need for Lesbians to Act on Aging" (1998, JIGS–*The Journal of Interdisciplinary Gender Studies*). She is a member of the board for the Australian Centre for Lesbian and Gay Research (ACLGR).

About the Contributors

John Connors is Lecturer in Psychology at Charles Sturt University, Australia. He graduated with a Bachelor of Arts with First Class Honours in Psychology, and was later awarded a Master of Arts degree for his research in the area of hypnosis. His dissertation for the degree of Master of Letters investigated decision-making in hypothetical situations involving possible health risks. He is a member of the Society of Australasian Social Psychologists. His research interests include attitudes to people to people living with HIV/AIDS and gender differences in body esteem. He has published a number of journal articles on the relationship between beliefs and attitudes to people living with HIV/AIDS.

Tania Ferfolja is completing her PhD in sociology at the University of New South Wales, Sydney, Australia. Her dissertation is on lesbian experiences of teaching in high schools and focuses on the multiple silences that operate in schools and which serve to marginalize lesbian experiences. She is currently Lecturer in the Learning Center at the University of New South Wales. Her research interests include sexuality, education, equity and diversity. She has published internationally in prestigious journals and has lectured on, and presented at numerous conferences in, this area. Tania is currently on the Board of Directors of the Australian Center for Lesbian and Gay Research.

Max Hopwood is a Research Officer at the National Centre in HIV Social Research at the University of New South Wales, Sydney, Australia. His research interests include illicit drug use and sexual practice in both gay and mainstream communities. Max's recent work explores gay men's illicit drug use within inner-Sydney gay precincts, and the injection of methadone syrup among people on oral methadone maintenance treatment in Sydney. Currently he is conducting a study of people living with hepatitis C and their experience of diagnosis, disclosure and discrimination.

Jude Irwin is Chair, Department of Social Work, Social Policy and Sociology, University of Sydney, Australia. She is a past Director of the Australian Center for Lesbian and Gay Research (ACLGR) and is currently a Board Member of the center. She is an appointed community member of the Council on Violence Against Women in New South Wales (NSW), Australia, and is a member of the NSW Child Death Review Team. She has practiced, researched and written extensively in the areas of violence against women and gay and lesbian issues, including the report *The Pink Ceiling Is Too Low: Workplace Experiences of Lesbians, Gay Men and Transgender People*.

Mairwen K. Jones is Lecturer in the School of Behavioural and Community Health Sciences at the University of Sydney. Mairwen completed an Honours Class 1 degree in psychology in 1992 and received the prestigious Australian Psychological Society Award for being placed equal first in the year. She completed her doctoral studies in 1997. Mairwen's main areas of research include human sexuality and the nature, origin and treatment of anxiety. She has presented at numerous conferences and published widely. Mairwen has been Acting Director of the University of Sydney's Anxiety Disorders Clinic and is currently Co-Director of the Australian Center for Gay and Lesbian Research.

Cynthia D. Nelson is Senior Lecturer at the English Language Study Skills Assistance Center at the University of Technology, Sydney. She has a Master's degree in Teaching English as a Second Language (ESL) (University of Washington, USA) and a PhD in Applied Linguistics (Macquarie University, Australia). Her dissertation investigated sexual identities in ESL. She has presented numerous conference papers on language education and academic writing, and has published her research in international, refereed journals such as *TESOL: Teachers of English to Speakers of Other Languages Quarterly*.

Kathleen Quinlivan is in the final stages of her PhD, which explores what is possible in terms of affirming sexual diversity in two New Zealand secondary schools. She teaches part time in the Education Department at Canterbury University in Christchurch, New Zealand, and operates a vocational mentoring project for LGBT youth. Kathleen has had recent work published with Shane Town in *A Dangerous Knowing: Sexuality Pedagogy And Popular Culture* (1999), edited by Debbie Epstein and James Sears. She has an upcoming article in *Queer in New Zealand* (2001), edited by Lynne Alice and Lynne Star (Dunmore Press).

Kerry H. Robinson is Senior Lecturer in sociology in the School of Education and Early Childhood Studies at the University of Western Sydney, Australia, where she teaches in the areas of sociology, difference and social justice. She has a PhD in sociology from the University of New South Wales, Australia. Her dissertation was completed in 1996 and investigated sexual harassment issues in secondary schooling. She is a Board member of the Australian Center for Lesbian and Gay Research. Her research interests include gender and sexual identity issues in education. She has published in prestigious international journals and presented at numerous conferences in this area.

Teresa Savage lives in Sydney and works as a librarian in public health.

Gerard Sullivan completed his PhD in sociology at the University of Hawaii, and currently teaches in the Faculty of Education at the University of Sydney. He is a member of the Australian Center for Lesbian and Gay Research. His recent work includes three books (coedited with Peter Jackson) published by Haworth Press: *Multicultural Queer: Australian Narratives* (1999), *Lady Boys, Tom Boys, Rent Boys: Male and Female Homosexualities in Contemporary Thailand* (1999), and *Lesbian and Gay Asia: Culture, Identity, Community* (2001).

Shane Town died in early 2000. Prior to his death, he was Lecturer in the Teacher Education Department at Victoria University in Wellington, New Zealand. Shane's PhD was the first New Zealand research to document the experiences of young gay men in schools. Shane was instrumental in establishing the national organization of lesbian and gay teachers, G.L.E.E (Gays and Lesbians Everywhere in Education), in the early 1990s. This organization acted as a lobby group to raise awareness of the issues faced by lesbian and gay students and teachers in schools and developed initiatives in order to create more inclusive schools.

∞ ALL HARRINGTON PARK PRESS BOOKS
AND JOURNALS ARE PRINTED
ON CERTIFIED ACID-FREE PAPER

Preface

Education systems are in a critical position to challenge the discrimination and inequality that is shown towards gays and lesbians from the wider community. More often, though, these systems are engaged with the constitution and perpetuation of this discrimination, reinforcing it through overt and covert discriminatory practices that result in the silencing and marginalization of lesbian and gay issues and identities. Lesbian and gay identities are often stereotyped, pathologized, and "othered" through myths and misinformation that can have various consequences, including violence, harassment, depression, alienation, suicide, and leaving education early. Such issues can have a crucial impact, in both the long and short term, on the social and personal well-being of lesbian and gay youth, teachers, and educators. As such, the papers in this collection aim to increase awareness in relation to lesbian and gay issues in education, demonstrating the importance for parents, employers, educational administrators, teacher educators, and teachers to reevaluate their policies and pedagogical practices in an effort to create a more egalitarian and just environment. Educators can play a crucial role in challenging discourses that foster hatred, discrimination, and fear around sexual difference.

Most of the papers in this compilation were originally presented at a conference in December 1998, organized by the Australian Center for Lesbian and Gay Research, a center affiliated with the University of Sydney, Australia. The collection focuses on a number of key issues relevant to homophobia and heterosexism in education and in society more broadly. Although these papers have an Australian and New Zealand context, they also highlight issues that are of major social and educational concern internationally.

Homophobia and heterosexism and the various forms of resistance employed by individuals and institutions are the central themes that form the basis of the discussions and create a cohesive collection of pa-

[Haworth co-indexing entry note]: "Preface." Robinson, Kerry H., Jude Irwin, and Tania Ferfolja. Co-published simultaneously in *Journal of Gay & Lesbian Social Services* (Harrington Park Press, an imprint of The Haworth Press, Inc.) Vol. 14, No. 2, 2002, pp. xxiii-xxv; and: *From Here to Diversity: The Social Impact of Lesbian and Gay Issues in Education in Australia and New Zealand* (ed: Kerry H. Robinson, Jude Irwin, and Tania Ferfolja) Harrington Park Press, an imprint of The Haworth Press, Inc., 2002, pp. xvii-xix. Single or multiple copies of this article are available for a fee from The Haworth Document Delivery Service [1-800-HAWORTH, 9:00 a.m. - 5:00 p.m. (EST). E-mail address: getinfo@haworthpressinc.com].

pers. There are eight articles in this collection that incorporate an eclectic range of theoretical perspectives which interweave the key themes of homophobia and heterosexism and the social implications on individuals across a number of educational contexts.

One of the main issues explored is the link between the social construction of gender, sexual identity, and homophobia in high schools. Town in his paper explores this in relation to the impact of hegemonic masculinity on the choices of young men. He highlights the often limited options that the schooling context offers around masculine identities and suggests that increasing the definitions of what it means to be male is crucial to counteracting homophobia and enhancing the lives of young men. Similarly, Quinlivan examines the representations of sexuality and gender that are available to young women within a single-sex secondary school. This paper incorporates a discussion of the normalization of heterosexuality and the perceived abnormality of same-sex desire constructed in classroom practices. Savage, from a different perspective, reflects on her experiences as a lesbian mother dealing with the education system in order to optimize her children's educational opportunities and, by doing this, tries to counteract potential harassment. Nelson, who utilizes queer theory and poststructuralist concepts, also emphasizes the need to explore the ways in which a variety of sexual identities are negotiated through daily interactions and highlights how this can be useful in working with students from language backgrounds other than English. These papers all have major social implications for the well-being of gays and lesbians and the importance of developing positive understandings of difference. Hence, reinforcing that education has the potential to be a catalyst for change, particularly around social definitions of gender and sexual identities.

Robinson and Ferfolja address teacher training and, by extension, workplace issues, focusing on their experiences of pre-service teachers' homophobic resistance to dealing with lesbian and gay issues in schooling. They stress the importance of addressing homophobia in schools in order to counteract the negative social consequences of discrimination and harassment. Homophobia and its impact on individuals in the workforce is also explored by Irwin, whose collaborative research into this area explicates the issues confronting gay men and lesbians who work in the education system. This is followed by an article by Hopwood and Connors which explores the university context investigating the possible contributing factors to predicting homophobia amongst university students in a rural community. Their paper concludes that students from particular disciplines hold more negative attitudes to lesbians and gay men, highlighting a need for greater anti-homophobic strategies in the university curriculum. The recognition of possible predictors of homophobia has implications for broader social policies and practices.

Finally, the last paper in this series addresses the implication of social and legal policy on educational initiatives and the resultant effect on lesbian and gay individuals in education and in society more broadly. Jones and Sullivan's paper provides a discussion on the perspectives and societal definitions of homophobia as either pathology or as a social prejudice. These authors argue that it is important to understand homophobia and its processes in order to challenge it.

Kerry H. Robinson
Jude Irwin
Tania Ferfolja

Acknowledgments

We would like to thank the Australian Center for Lesbian and Gay Research for their support with this project as well as the contributions made by the peer reviewers of the papers in this collection.

We would also like to dedicate this collection to one of the contributors, Dr. Shane Town, who died before the completion of this project. Shane was a gifted and inspired teacher and a warm and generous man who supported and supervised a wide range of students and who undertook work in the area of both sexualities and schooling. At both a practical and an intellectual level, Shane played an important role in working towards challenging heteronormativity in New Zealand's educational institutions and in creating more inclusive schools for lesbian, gay, and bisexual students. Shane's death is a great loss to both the educational and lesbian and gay communities in which he worked.

Kerry H. Robinson
Jude Irwin
Tania Ferfolja

Playing with Fire: (Homo)sexuality and Schooling in New Zealand

Shane Town

SUMMARY. This paper explores the ways in which representations of masculinity and sexuality in schools operate to reinforce limited opportunities for male students in New Zealand. Data were gathered from in-depth interviews with ten young gay men and focus group interviews with seven young gay men. The discussion demonstrates how schools currently restrict opportunities for young gay men to explore masculinity in relation to their sexuality and highlights the ways in which schools support and reinforce binaries of heterosexuality/homosexuality in terms of normality and abnormality. The paper raises important implications for gender identity and equity in schooling. *[Article copies available for a fee from The Haworth Document Delivery Service: 1-800-HAWORTH. E-mail address: <getinfo@haworthpressinc.com> Website: <http://www.HaworthPress.com> © 2002 by The Haworth Press, Inc. All rights reserved.]*

KEYWORDS. Homosexuality, schooling, masculinities, New Zealand, heteronormativity, homophobia, heterosexism, gay, students, violence

---

Prior to his death, Shane Town, PhD, was working with the Teacher Education Department at Victoria University, New Zealand.

[Haworth co-indexing entry note]: "Playing with Fire: (Homo)sexuality and Schooling in New Zealand." Town, Shane. Co-published simultaneously in *Journal of Gay & Lesbian Social Services* (Harrington Park Press, an imprint of The Haworth Press, Inc.) Vol. 14, No. 2, 2002, pp. 1-15; and: *From Here to Diversity: The Social Impact of Lesbian and Gay Issues in Education in Australia and New Zealand* (ed: Kerry H. Robinson, Jude Irwin, and Tania Ferfolja) Harrington Park Press, an imprint of The Haworth Press, Inc., 2002, pp. 1-15. Single or multiple copies of this article are available for a fee from The Haworth Document Delivery Service [1-800-HAWORTH, 9:00 a.m. - 5:00 p.m. (EST). E-mail address: getinfo@haworthpressinc.com].

In recent years educational discourses on gender have begun to focus on relationships between boys and learning, masculinity and male violence. The controversies surrounding masculinity and schooling can be seen reflected in a variety of media through programs created to address bullying. Television advertisement campaigns, such as those sponsored by Telecom and fronted by All Black heroes like football player Michael Jones, are being promoted as ways to reduce bullying and violence in schools. These programs are accompanied by a significant growth in the number of newspaper articles that focus on boys' underachievement in numeracy and literacy tests, their overrepresentation in school suspensions, and the need for more positive role models in schools and father figures in families.

Prior to the developing "male focus" identified above, the last two decades witnessed considerable attention being played to issues of gender from female perspectives. Up until the 1990s, gender in educational discourse had been seen and understood by policy makers and teachers to be synonymous with girls or women. The 1970s witnessed a focus on girls. Discourses on a number of levels surrounded "girls can do anything" and schools encouraged female participation in "nontraditional areas" in math, science, and technology. The 1980s witnessed a shift toward gender inclusion in curriculum documents that suggests that women's roles in history and society needed to be made explicit within the classroom. By the 1990s girls are not only participating more, they are achieving, on average, better than boys.

The "success" of girls in schooling in the 1990s and the increasing acknowledgment of failure of boys in literacy and numeracy is being used to challenge the attention and status given to girls in schooling. However, opponents of these views identify the continuing disparities in post school and employment as signs that schools and political and economic systems continue to discriminate against women. The debates as they currently stand and are played out in media and educational discourse create an either/or binary; girls or boys must succeed, girls or boys need special treatment, girls or boys require special programs and resources.

The approach outlined above which reinforces either/or binaries fails to identify the complexity underlying the ways in which gender is constituted and represented in schooling. Connell (1995, p. 207) suggests that we need to analyze the hegemonic nature of masculinity, to question the usefulness of making generalizations about "boys as a bloc," and to focus research on achieving a better knowledge of "how far schools can affect masculinity and its enactment."

Seidman (1993, p. 129) suggested that liberation theory (of the 1970s and 1980s) "confronted a dialectic of identity and difference that revolved around straight/gay and man/woman polarities. Currently these oppositions are multiplied a hundredfold as we introduce differences along the dimensions of race, ethnicity, gender, age, sexual act, class, lifestyle and locale." In a sense, the problems of identity posed by poststructuralist writers and queer theorists such as Seidman (1993) have seen us move from the "big" stories of class, race, culture, and gender to focus on the "little" stories of the individual. An individual's perceptions of truth and the proliferation of possible subjectivities these personal truths give rise to have become significant components of research and writing in the areas of sociology and education. In light of the above, issues of masculinity and schooling become much more complex and the search for truths becomes a search for multiple ways of understanding the experience of young males in our schools. Davies (1993) suggests that an understanding of young boys' struggles to organize their subjectivities to fit powerful male positions in schools and communities is a useful beginning to understanding their experience and behavior.

One of the truths, which have almost without fail been silenced within masculinity discourses, is the positions of young gay men. As some writers (Connell, 1995; Mac An Ghaill, 1994) suggest, no analysis of masculinity can be achieved without consideration of the roles homophobia and heterosexism play in producing and maintaining hegemonic structures. Seldom are gay male voices heard. There has been little research and writing in education from gay male perspectives which explores the ways in which gay men come to understand themselves as male within institutions which actively work to promote heterosexuality and macho behaviors as the only ways of being.

The emergence in the 1990s of queer theory within sociological and literary disciplines reconceptualizes gender and sexuality as fluid, unstable and destabilizing (Jagose, 1996; Warner, 1993). The hegemonic nature of heterosexuality, the power of heteronormative discourses, their relationship and intersections with gender have become a focus for attempting to understand the experiences of lesbian/gay/bisexual/transgendered youth. An exploration of the intersections of sexuality and gender has also provided the impetus to reconceptualize normalization processes and their role in policing gender. Queer educationalists and researchers such as Britzman (1995) have begun to explore the ways in which tenets of queer theory can be applied within classrooms. As Quinlivan and Town (1995) suggest, "taking queer out of the realm of the academy and adult political spheres and into the world of youth and education provides opportunities for youth to move beyond the minoritizing discourses which currently frame their [lesbian and gay youths' experience of] schooling." Heteronormativity is like the air that we breathe (Town, 1999). Placing homosexuality within a wider and more *universalizing discourse of difference* is one way to begin to address the needs of both heterosexual and nonheterosexual youth.

The purpose of this paper is to explore the ways in which schooling currently restricts opportunities for young gay men to explore masculinity in relation to their sexuality. Secondly, the paper involves examining the ways in which schools support and reinforce binaries of straight, masculine, normal, accepted, and worshipped; and gay, feminine, abnormal, unacceptable, and abhorrent. The paper draws upon material gathered from several sources that include: (1) Interviews with ten young gay men about their schooling undertaken in 1994 as part of my doctoral studies. (2) Data gathered from a series of three focus group interviews with seven young gay men and eight lesbians. These focus groups were held during the production in 1997 of a professional development video to provide information and constructive ideas about how schools could become more inclusive of the needs of gay/lesbian/bisexual/transgendered students. It is aimed at both students and teachers/administrators in intermediate and secondary schools. (3) Data from Understanding Learning and Teaching Project 2, Canterbury University, which reflects the experience of a young male in primary school has also been used.

The first section of the paper focuses on exploring the limited subject positions available to young men throughout their schooling. The second section examines the effects these subjectivities have on the way in which the young gay men respond to, resist, and struggle against heteronormative and masculine discourses which frame their experience. The third section explores how opportunities to voice their stories and explore ways of reconstituting masculinity as young men can create possibilities for males, straight and gay and bisexual, masculine and feminine, to perceive themselves as they choose rather than as society and schooling define. Illustrative quotes from interview and focus group participants will be used in the sections that follow. The names of all participants have been changed to preserve their anonymity.

LEARNING TO PLAY IN THE FOOTBALL TEAM

Schools play a significant role in teaching males to be heterosexual and masculine. For the seventeen young men who have been involved in two research studies (Town, 1996), learning to "reject" their gayness was an important part of their socialization into the masculine world. Rich (1980) suggests we live in worlds defined by compulsory heterosexuality; for these young men compulsory heterosexuality was inevitably and inherently tied up with compulsory masculinity. Compulsory representations of masculinity within school environments were achieved through a variety of subtle and hegemonic practices such as: defeminization and masculinization, dis/ease and pathologization, and deterrence and violence.

Defeminization, Diversion, and Masculinization

Schools as sites in which control is maintained over sexuality and masculinity is not a new idea. The Victorian era saw the development of two myths (amongst others) in response to the moral panics in public schools of the late nineteenth century. The first myth is that to keep a boy's mind pure and free from temptation it was best to "toughen him up." The second was to ensure he learned to fight off "depraved emotional tendencies" (Hickson, 1995). These myths still pervade the way many parents approach their sons and many schools (especially boys' schools) approach the education of their male students. Somehow it is thought that if you encourage a young boy not to display his emotions and to reject anything that can be perceived as feminine then you will ensure he is heterosexual. As Andrew, an interview participant, said, at a certain age it became unacceptable for him to exhibit anything other than heterosexual behavior and he had to learn to "reject his gayness." As he says:

> . . . I wish I was [heterosexual] kind of thing . . . it would make things a bit easier . . . at an earlier age I embraced my gayness . . . but I learned to reject it. (Andrew, age 19)

For Peter, a student in a traditional boys' boarding school, sexuality was controlled through limiting spare time in which it would be possible for him to have immoral or depraved thoughts.

> . . . it would be the attitude from the executives at school that boys aren't engaging in sex at the moment . . . you know . . . playing rugby hard, cricket hard, studying hard and that sort of thing . . . (Peter, aged 21)

Peter's reflections on the diversion tactics utilized by schools to discourage sexual thoughts and behaviors are also experienced by boys in their primary schooling. Davies (1993) identified primary schooling as a site where young boys learn how to be heterosexual men. The textual narratives contained within fairy tales and adventure stories that operate as the basis of knowledge for boys on how they should constitute themselves as men reinforce ideas of heroism and toughness as essential masculine ingredients. Primary school classrooms and playgrounds are sites where young boys learn the lived narratives available to them (Davies, 1993). Boys in schools learn to be "tough," learn not to cry and learn to suppress their emotions. One of the tests which boys need to pass in their peer group to be accepted as fully recognized males is to receive verbal and physical abuse "like a man." Although the purposes of the abuse that Sam at age nine received are unclear and ambiguous to him, he realized that his reaction to the abuse was important for his status in his peer group. As he said in his interview, he "couldn't just stand there and (then) walk off":

> Sam: He really gets me angry. I couldn't just stand there and let him just say them, "you big dick" and all that and start shouting at me and throwing balls at me, calling me "you moron," "homo" and all that.
>
> Interviewer: They're pretty hard words.
>
> Sam: I couldn't just stand there and walk off and be behind me saying all these words, I just couldn't get away from it.
>
> Interviewer: What does he mean by the word moron?
>
> Sam: I don't know.
>
> Interviewer: What about "you big dick" when they say things like that? What do you think they're trying to mean?
>
> Sam: They are trying to say to me, oh I don't know what they're trying to mean, but it means something and I don't like it.

Sam goes on in the interview to explain how the intervention of his teacher was not enough to prevent the verbal abuse from continuing and, in fact, made it more problematic in further compromising his position.

Sam further explained that his grandfather, his father, and his stepfather had told him that if he just "punched" the other boys, it would stop. Ultimately, he felt he was left with little alternative than to retaliate physically by "punching" one of the boys picking on him. In doing so it seems he was able to establish a "heroic" and dominant position within his peer group. The boy whom he punched indicated that he was only calling Sam names because another boy was making him do it.

> Sam: The teacher had a real good talk to him and then this time I got really upset and this time he got sent to _____ and a friend. Cause when I punched him, I punched one of the boys. I winded him in the stomach . . . he went outside with me and said "it wasn't my fault, I didn't get him upset" and I said "yes it was, you were saying those words to me" and he said "[the other boy] was making me." Well nobody *makes* you so.

The links here between homophobic discourses surrounding the interchange between the boys ("you homo") and the discourses of male violence ("[the other boy] was making me") within primary schools is evident. It seems there is always another boy who forces the offender to act, highlighting the hegemonic nature of both heterosexuality and homophobia, which revolve around processes of normalization and defeminization. Sam knew that the school rules said violence was wrong; however, upon the advice of older males in his life and his own experience he learned that violence was the only way to change the behavior of his male peer group. Already for nine-year-old Sam, violence was preferable to accepting the abuse and the positioning he did not even understand, that of "homo."

By the age of 19, as Alistair said in the focus group interviews, there is no longer any need to wonder as Sam does at the meaning of the verbal and physical abuse inherent in his peer group interchanges, it is "like society teaches you."

> It's very hard to explain . . . it's like society teaches you that to be a man you have to have a wife, and you have to be a jock, and you have to be able to take your alcohol and drive fast, and all these things. And the only boys that have all this sort of thing are boys who are straight, and play rugby, or sport. And so you think, well, to fit in to that I have to have all those things, to be a proper member of society . . . (Alistair, aged 19)

Dis/ease and Pathologization

The inevitability of public presumptions of heterosexuality and expected male norms of behavior provided the opportunity and the necessity for the majority of young men in the studies to maintain a heterosexual public identity in the face of a private knowledge of their (homo)sexuality. To "speak" publicly of their sexuality and to challenge a century of silence about (homo)sexuality would as suggested by Foucault (1976) require the "striking" of a "different pose" on the part of the young men. To adopt a position outside of the "norm" would have led to the young men being victimized and isolated within their peer group. The limited information and stereotypes of gay men that the young men received as children had reinforced their perceptions that public acknowledgment was not possible and that they did not fit the stereotype and therefore could not be gay. As William said:

> I thought they (gay men) were child molesting people that went out in the community and were flashers that . . . grabbed children off the street . . . public toilet kind of people . . . go and hang around in a dark park and wait for someone to pick up . . . a very negative dark image. (William, aged 19)

The discourse of homosexual as dis/eased sexual predator was used to instill fear and lead to the rejection in young boys of their own (homo)sexual feelings. Similarly, it was the perception of other participants that gay men led secretive lives and this knowledge contributed to their decision not to disclose their "true" sexuality to others. The lack of visibility of masculine gay male images reinforced the participants' feelings of dis/ease concerning (homo)sexuality. As Sasha suggests, secrecy leads to suspicion.

> I suppose I had never met anyone who was gay . . . I suppose it comes from that feeling that if there were gay men out there they must live secretive lives . . . and I'm suspicious of things which aren't open. (Sasha, aged 19)

Pathologization messages were also received from within the official school curricula. For James, education concerning HIV/AIDS in his school had helped reinforce his belief that (homo)sexuality was directly related to this disease and that to be gay meant dying of AIDS at a young age.

> I shut it out because I didn't know what I was going to go through, what was going to become of me, was I going to get AIDS when I was twenty . . . I just didn't want to face up to things . . . (James, aged 18)

Deterrence and Violence

The perceptions of the young men of the inherently violent nature of their schooling were apparent when they were asked to explore their experience of homophobia within their school environments and communities. For some participants, such as Andy, being involved in physically violent situations was a part of their schooling and a significant part of their ability to project and maintain public, heterosexual, and masculine images. For others, such as Richard, the almost-daily physical violence he was subjected to led him to truant for twenty per cent of his secondary schooling. For the majority of young men a realization that coming out would endanger their physical and emotional well-being reinforced their decisions not to disclose their sexuality at school. The effects on the participants of managing their identities in hostile schools and communities have been documented (Massachusetts State Education Daprtment, 1996; Quinlivan & Town, 1999; Sears, 1992) and include suicide ideation, depression, dysfunctional peer and family relationships, and alcohol and drug use.

Connell (1995) and Mac An Ghaill (1994) identified the peer group as a site in which many of our "acceptable" gender behaviors are taught, learned, and monitored. Homophobic abuse in schools and classrooms was used both directly and indirectly to police acceptable masculine behaviors among the young men in the studies.

All of the participants in both studies experienced and/or witnessed verbal abuse concerning (homo)sexuality in their schools. Often the verbal abuse was accompanied by threats of physical violence. As Andrew and James suggested, the list of abuse terms for suspected (homo)sexuals was creative and felt "endless," used to police the boundaries along the binary of strong male inclusion (1st XV) and weak male/female exclusion.

> . . . nasty things like ankle snatchers, donut makers . . . the list goes on . . . tongue in groove, pooh pushers . . . lots of things, it is endless. (Andrew, aged 19)

> Name-calling . . . like faggot and things like that and say how can you have sex with a man and all that kind of stuff . . . but yeah . . . basically most of them were male 1st XV type . . . I didn't really like them. (James, aged 18)

Sears (1992) identified the historical and cultural constructions of boyhood effeminacy which link (homo)sexuality with feminine behaviors and sensibilities. The internal struggle for masculine and heterosexual identities is mirrored by external attempts to police gender/sexual norms and behaviors through bullying in schools and communities. Bullying among boys and men in both physical and verbal forms often revolves around misogynist language and behavior (Connell, 1995).

The participants who conformed sufficiently to the masculine ideals of the school environment and deflected abuse were witness to the effects it had on others, confirming their own fears about their sexuality and reinforcing decisions not to disclose their (homo)sexuality publicly. For Andy, who was a member of his private boy's school 1st XV, the internal and private struggle for a masculine identity left him feeling at risk of uncovering some sort of "trizzie queen" in himself that was in opposition to his carefully constructed masculine, rugby playing, heterosexual image.

> I just didn't know whether I was going to become some trizzie queen or something like that I'd been trying to cover up . . . suddenly I thought this monster was going to emerge and I would turn into Julian Clary or something. (Andy, aged 21)

Andy's private internal struggle to compensate for his (homo)sexual feelings was also played out publicly in the form of collusion with his peer group in homophobic physical and verbal abuse of boys identified as gay and/or different.

> I guess if somebody else was targeted (I did collude in homophobic situations) . . . I guess I felt like Tommy Walter, tell on him but don't tell on me. No I was a coward and I feel ashamed now . . . it was run with the foxes, hunt with the hounds. (Andy, aged 21)

In attempting to create a masculine and acceptable identity, Andy had little alternative but to play along with his peer group. The internal fears he had of becoming isolated and identified as a "poofter" or "faggot" ensured he supported behavior, which he felt uncomfortable about and "ashamed" of. The costs of not performing the masculine and male rites of violence upon other male students would ensure, as Andy says, losing not only his friends but also his status in his peer group, a "fate," at the time, "worse than death."

> Oh losing my friends, which would have happened. Well there was one individual in our class who did not come into the common room after a certain incident and . . . he was more or less ostracized by the greater student population . . . I saw the same fate for me being found out, I don't know possibly worse because I had a higher public profile in the school, throughout the school I had to stand up at assemblies and I was visible . . . I think that being found out would have been a fate worse than death. (Andy, aged 21)

For Richard, who experienced physical and verbal violence meted out by other boys in an attempt to consolidate their masculine image, school was an unpleasant and unsafe place to be. The abuse in this instance was supported by Richard's male Physical Education (P.E.) teacher, who used his weight as an object of derision to further marginalize him from within his peer group. As Richard says, the intolerance of difference in schools, publicly displaying physical or emotional weakness rather than just sexuality per se, was what led to him being picked on.

> Richard: . . . they just called me faggot because I was fat . . . I think. Oh and I was teased by one of the teachers as well um . . . one of the P.E. teachers . . . called me stubby; he said, "hey stubby" and everyone laughed . . . laughed because of that so they called me stubby from then on. I used to bunk P.E.
>
> Interviewer: I'm not surprised . . . was it just verbal abuse?
>
> Richard: . . . biking to school is when it would happen . . . I'd meet some people in the bike stands . . . the class would be in and in the break . . . oh everyone would just be teasing me . . . in PE . . . every time I used to get named different things . . . if you played cricket and missed a ball or something else they called you a faggot . . . yeah it was really horrendous but . . . I think I can't really get in touch with that because of the lack of distance I have from it . . . because I know I was real . . . really sad . . . (Richard, aged 17)

Gay and Rucked to Death

Young males aged between 15 and 24 in New Zealand are killing themselves at a rate of 38 per hundred thousand. These figures do not account for those who wrap their cars around lampposts or drive off country roads. Remafedi, French, Story, Resnick and Blum (1998) found in a population based study that young gay men were seven times more likely to attempt suicide than their heterosexual counterparts. Discourses surrounding youth suicide focus on the dysfunctional nature of the individual or their family, seeking to link suicide to pathological behavior and personal attributes. In doing so, researchers, government agencies, and policy makers exploring issues of suicide in communities perhaps fail to take into account the significance of how masculinity and sexuality influence the ways in which young men conceptualize and negotiate their subjectivities in relation to others.

Sears (1992) and others (Quinlivan, 1996; Remafedi et al., 1998; Uribe & Harbeck, 1992) indicate that often the internal despair carried by a gay/lesbian/bisexual/transgendered youth is kept private from their families, communities, and peer group for fear of reprisal, loss of family support and friendships. It is an individual youth's internalization of the experiences of homophobia from their parents, their friends, their communities and their schools which translates into depression, low self-esteem, and sadly, suicide by some.

It should be noted that none of the seventeen participants across the two studies attempted or succeeded in committing suicide. However, six of the young men reported that they had thought about suicide and four knew other gay males who had attempted suicide. Andy and Richard, who spoke at length in their interviews about considering suicide, said they did so for quite different reasons. Andy perceived suicide fitted his romanticized notion of the "heroic male," and, although tragic, in his view would have enabled him to retain the public and high status position he had achieved within his peer group and his family. The internalization of the homophobia Andy participated in paralleled the struggle he was having in attaining the masculine ideals of family and peer group. As he stated, public knowledge of his (homo)sexuality would have "embarrassed" his family and at the time he was unable to conceive of a future in which he could be "happy" and "gay":

> Years. It just always, always, always seemed like what was going to happen. It was always in the back of my mind that I was going to kill myself at some stage. I was hoping I was going to kill myself

> before people found out . . . I didn't want to embarrass my family which is what I thought would happen when people found out I was gay–if they found out I was gay. But I never ever thought I was going to get to the stage where I am now. I never knew that it was possible to live and be happy as a gay person. And as soon as I realized that I was a gay person it seemed completely impossible to be happy. And because I knew that I felt that I couldn't be happy, or I felt that I couldn't make anybody else happy. Anybody else I care about happy. Yeah, I thought that it was the best thing to do . . . So it seemed quite a normal thing to do. But it was no big deal. I was going to as soon as I got the courage . . . (Andy, aged 21)

For Richard, however, suicide was perceived as a way out of the abuse he was experiencing in his school from both adults and his peer group. He saw his possible suicide in terms of the revenge it would exact on those who abused him and the benefits it could bring to others in his position, through making public the pain and humiliation he was experiencing.

> I know I used to tell myself how it could hurt . . . how it could hurt other people and basically that I did . . . I think I believed in myself enough that . . . if I did it then I'm just . . . it's just a waste . . . like no one would ever know what I'm really like and I could die and they would only ever remember people picked on me and sure it might be good for people after me who were picked on but . . . um . . . it wouldn't change for me and I wouldn't know what was next so I wouldn't benefit from my own suicide. (Richard, aged 17)

Finding My Voice at the Bottom of the Scrum

> After the interview last week I felt much better about myself . . . it was all brought out into the open . . . it has gone back a bit but I still feel better about myself . . . (Zak, aged 19)

On average, the participants identified as gay to themselves between the ages of ten and fourteen. However, the average length of time between acknowledging their sexuality to themselves and telling another person was approximately three to four years. This period of silence and fear was problematic for the young men as they attempted to negotiate the meanings of a sexuality that forced them to adopt subject positions that were anything but powerful (Davies, 1993).

The interview/filming process provided one of the few opportunities the young men had to explore their sexual identities. As such, the process required the participants to reflect on their perceptions of their place in the world, as males and as young gay men. For the participants the opportunity to explore issues of identity as an adolescent and as an integral part of their schooling needed to be provided in an environment where one was not seen as deficient. Young men seldom see, hear and/or experience images of male identity other than heroic and heterosexual within schools.

Britzman (1995) suggests that teachers need to provide opportunities for children to be able to explore their fears. A queer pedagogical approach which positions gender and sexuality in more fluid terms could possibly have enabled a youth like Andy to see beyond his fears of becoming a "trizzie queen." Perhaps the role models and stories which should be encouraged in schools to complement rugby heroes and adventurers are those which would disrupt the binaries. Gay rugby players, drag queens, cross dressing policemen, and gay, lesbian, bisexual youth confound traditional binaries of powerful/powerless, straight/gay, male/female. These "little" stories in the telling have the potential to disrupt and re/present the hegemonic texts which guide the lived narratives of young boys as they struggle to make meaning of their masculinity.

The participants in the two studies found the interview and filming processes helpful in that they allowed them to identify issues that still needed resolving in terms of their gay, masculine, and feminine identities. Talking about their sexuality and their understandings of masculinity enabled the participants to deconstruct their experience and challenge the heteronormative nature of their schooling. This deconstructive process is significant as it demonstrates the importance of providing venues in which youth can explore possibilities and where limitations and judgments are not imposed (Town, 1996).

As Davies (1993) suggested, providing reading and writing experiences in classrooms which enable children to identify silences and disrupt certainties of gender and sexuality "opens up new possibilities" for identity work in schools. Britzman (1995) suggested that teachers and schools need to encourage children to study what it is "they cannot bear to know," to "think the unthinkable" and to "read against the text." Creating activities and utilizing resources that enable young males to explore subject positions other than "heroic" and in relation to themselves as young males could perhaps benefit all participants in the education system.

REFERENCES

Britzman, D. (1995). Is there a queer pedagogy? Or, stop reading straight. *Educational Theory*, *45* (2), 151-165.

Connell, R.W. (1995). *Masculinities*. Great Britain: Polity Press.

Davies, B. (1993). *Shards of glass: Children reading and writing beyond gendered identities*. New Jersey: Hampton Press.

Foucault, M. (1976). *History of sexuality. Vol. 1*. Great Britain: Penguin.

Hickson, A. (1995). *The poisoned bowl: Sex and the public school*. Great Britain: Duckworth Press.

Jagose, A. (1996). *Queer theory*. Dunedin: University of Otago Press.

Mac An Ghaill, M. (1994). *The making of men: Masculinities, sexualities and schooling*. Buckingham: Open University Press.

Massachusetts State Education Department (1996). *1995 Youth risk behaviour study*. Boston: Massachusetts Education Department.

Quinlivan, K. (1996). "Claiming an identity they taught me to despise": Lesbian students respond to the regulation of same sex desire. *New Zealand Women's Studies Journal*, *12*, (2), 99-113.

Quinlivan, K., & Town, S.J.H. (1999). Queer as fuck? Exploring the potential of queer pedagogies in researching school experiences of lesbian and gay youth. In D. Epstein & J. Sears (Eds.), *A dangerous knowing: Sexuality, pedagogy and popular culture*. London: Cassell.

Remafedi, G., French, S., Story, M., Resnick, M., & Blum, R. (1998). The relationship between suicide risk and sexual orientation: Results of a population-based study. *American Journal of Public Health*, *88*, (1), January, 57-60.

Rich, A. (1980). Compulsory heterosexuality and lesbian existence. *Signs: Journal of Women in Culture and Society*, *5*, 631-60.

Sears, J. (1992). *Growing up gay in the South*. New York: Harrington Park Press.

Seidman, S. (1993). Identity and politics in a "Postmodern" gay culture: Some historical and conceptual notes. In Warner, M. (Ed.), *Fear of a queer planet*. (pp. 105-142). Minneapolis: University of Minnesota Press.

Town, S.J.H. (1999). Queer(y)ing masculinities. Faggots, fairies and the first fifteen. In H. Campbell & R. Law (Eds.), *Masculinities in Aotearoa/New Zealand*. Palmerston North: Dunmore Press.

Town, S.J.H. (1996). *Is it safe to come out yet? The impact of secondary schooling on the positive identity development of ten young gay men*. (ERIC Document Reproduction Service No. ED 395 262).

Uribe, V., & Harbeck, K. (1992). Addressing the needs of lesbian, gay, and bisexual youth: The origins of PROJECT 10 and school-based intervention. In K. Harbeck (Ed.), *Coming out of the classroom closet: Gay and lesbian students, teachers, and curricula*. New York: Harrington Park Press.

Warner, M. (1993). *Fear of a queer planet*. Minneapolis: University of Minnesota Press.

Whose Problem Is This? Queerying the Framing of Lesbian and Gay Secondary School Students Within "At Risk" Discourses

Kathleen Quinlivan

SUMMARY. This paper is concerned with how the needs of lesbian and gay youth are situated and defined in educational contexts and the intended and unintended consequences of framing their needs in particular ways. It is based on a case study of a senior college in New Zealand where a strategy for dealing with gay and lesbian youth was framed within a climate of market-driven educational reforms and where queer youth were viewed within the discourse of being "at risk." This enabled the school to promote itself as providing a caring and nurturing environment without jeopardizing its position in the marketplace. However, this strategy had the unfortunate consequences of re-pathologizing lesbian and gay students and constructing their sexuality as a personal problem. *[Article copies available for a fee from The Haworth Document Delivery Service: 1-800-HAWORTH. E-mail address: <getinfo@haworthpressinc.com> Website: <http://www.HaworthPress.com> © 2002 by The Haworth Press, Inc. All rights reserved.]*

Kathleen Quinlivan is affiliated with the Education Department, University of Canterbury, Private bag 4800, Christchurch, New Zealand (E-mail: k.quinlivan@educ.canterbury.ac.nz).

[Haworth co-indexing entry note]: "Whose Problem Is This? Queerying the Framing of Lesbian and Gay Secondary School Students Within 'At Risk' Discourses." Quinlivan, Kathleen. Co-published simultaneously in *Journal of Gay & Lesbian Social Services* (Harrington Park Press, an imprint of The Haworth Press, Inc.) Vol. 14, No. 2, 2002, pp. 17-31; and: *From Here to Diversity: The Social Impact of Lesbian and Gay Issues in Education in Australia and New Zealand* (ed: Kerry H. Robinson, Jude Irwin, and Tania Ferfolja) Harrington Park Press, an imprint of The Haworth Press, Inc., 2002, pp. 17-31. Single or multiple copies of this article are available for a fee from The Haworth Document Delivery Service [1-800-HAWORTH, 9:00 a.m. - 5:00 p.m. (EST). E-mail address: getinfo@haworthpressinc.com].

KEYWORDS. Lesbian, gay, students, schooling, at risk, queer theory, pathologization

INTRODUCTION

This article explores how one New Zealand high school attempted to meet the needs of its gay and lesbian students. The case study school, Riverside College,[1] adopted the primary strategy of framing the sexuality of self-identified individual students as a "barrier to learning" whose "anxiety about their sexuality," as the school principal explains it, could be addressed through the school's guidance counseling network. Situating the strategy within a climate of market-driven educational reforms, I suggest the approach enabled Riverside College to promote itself as providing a caring and nurturing environment without jeopardizing the school's position in the marketplace. The strategy did meet the needs of some individual self-identified lesbian and gay students and also moved in general directions towards raising an awareness of the issues which face bisexual youth in the school. However, it also had the unfortunate consequences of re-pathologizing lesbian and gay students and constructing their sexuality as a personal problem. I suggest that the approach limits the likelihood of Riverside College being able to address the heteronormative culture of the school, which, as Apple (1995) suggests, is the real underlying problem.

Research Design and Methodological Constraints

Riverside College is a state co-educational secondary school situated in a suburb of a large urban center. It has a stable enrollment of 700 students, comprising equal numbers of young women and men. Forty-eight full-time staff teach at the school. Describing the school as predominantly middle class and monocultural, the principal commented on a recent survey that indicated that 80% of the parents in those areas owned their own home and there was virtually no state housing. Over a third of the students travel from out of the area to attend the school. The principal also commented that Riverside was perceived to be the more traditional alternative to its more liberal competition.

Semi-structured interviews, field notes, and participant observations have been the forms of data collection. The interviews were based on a schedule constructed by me and viewed by the participants prior to their being interviewed. The scope of the interviews allowed the participants to explain what initiatives were currently in place to meet the needs of lesbian and gay youth in the school and describe the features of the school that made such initiatives possible there. Several of the participants also took the opportunity to discuss the limitations of the school's approaches. After the interviews had been undertaken, the transcripts were returned to the participants with follow-up questions requesting more detail and in some cases posing new questions. A report was given to the participants on completion of the project.

Face to face semi-structured interviews were undertaken with five participants who represented a range of perspectives within the school. Graeme was a heterosexual male 46-year-old school counselor who had 15 years' experience in the school. Ryan was a sixth form gay male student who was in his final year at school. James was the school principal, 53 years old, male and heterosexual; he had been at the school for twelve years. Richard was a 43-year-old openly gay male head of the math department who had been teaching for nine years at the school. Suzanne was a 43-year-old female economics teacher who has been teaching at Riverside for the last eight years and was reasonably open about being lesbian. Pseudonyms have been used for both the names of the school and the participants. In some cases details of the school and the participants have been blurred in order to further protect their confidentiality.

Access and communication difficulties which occurred while undertaking the research provided some insights into the tensions some schools experience in relation to meeting the needs of queer students. Documenting these difficulties provided insights into the nature and scope of the data I collected by illuminating key issues. I had earlier been refused access to undertake this study at another school on the basis that it would reflect negatively on the school's reputation to be seen as meeting the needs of lesbian and bisexual students and might adversely affect their projected enrollment numbers. This experience provided me with some understanding of the pressure schools are currently experiencing to compete with each other within the market-driven educational climate and the ways in which openly meeting the needs of queer youth could be perceived to compromise the position of the school in the educational marketplace.

Gaining access to Riverside College and negotiating access to the participants, especially the principal, proved to be a rather complex and confusing process. While the principal agreed to be interviewed, the onus was on the gay teacher to arrange the process. Richard felt that the principal was not keen to document the extent to which the school met the needs of lesbian, gay, and bisexual students but that there would have been pressure brought to bear on him by a range of staff if he had resisted.

It was also difficult for me to get responses from the principal both during and after the interview with him to questions concerning the issues which make it difficult for schools to attempt to meet the needs of lesbian, gay, and bisexual youth. I think the issues which emerged as part of the interview process illustrated some of the tensions which arise for schools as they juggle the roles of marketing themselves and building the image of their schools while at the same time being seen to attempt to meet the needs of lesbian and gay students (an initiative which it is perceived that many parents may feel uncomfortable about). In the case of Riverside College, this resulted in the principal in particular finding it more palatable to frame lesbian and gay students' sexuality as a personal deficit and "barrier to learning." The school is then seen as doing their utmost to meet students' individual "problems" by referring them to the school counselor for "help" with their sexuality. This approach enables the school to be seen as meeting students' individual needs, and does not adversely affect the position of the school in the educational marketplace.

Because I was able to talk to only one woman at the school and because I was unable to interview lesbian or bisexual students, their subjectivities were overshadowed by gay male perspectives. This situation is exacerbated by the fact that Richard, as a gay male teacher, has such a high profile in the school and, as such, the emphasis within the school is more on gay male sexuality. Added to which, it is primarily young gay men that Graeme, the guidance counselor, has worked with. In light of the fact that research shows lesbian students to be a largely invisible population in schools (Khayatt, 1994; Quinlivan, 1996), this silence does raise issues concerning the invisibility of lesbian and bisexual students at Riverside College. While an exploration of the silencing of lesbian and bisexual students at Riverside College is beyond the scope of this paper, it is worth noting that the participants tend to focus on gay male youth within "at risk" discourses and that lesbian and bisexual perspectives are frequently invisible.

Theoretical Frameworks

Drawing on queer post structuralist notions of sexual identity as an unstable, shifting, and evolving construct and on cultural reproduction theories, this paper explores the role that "at risk" schooling discourses play in marginalizing and abnormalizing representations of queer sexualities.

Institutions such as schools are important agents for the production and transmission of sexual beliefs and values. It is the representation of subjects in language organized by particular discursive systems, including schools, that positions subjects in relations of control, discipline, and moral regulation (Luke & Gore, 1992). Schools, then, play an active role in reproducing constructions of sexualities. They operate as cultural sites to reproduce understandings and practices about sexuality in both the formal and hidden curriculum. Recently educational research has begun to explore the ways in which sexual categories and the social practices which sustain them operate as discourses to construct and abnormalize representations of lesbian and gay sexuality within schools (Epstein & Johnson, 1998; Mac An Ghaill, 1994; Quinlivan & Town, 1999; Quinlivan, in press). Within the binary construction of heterosexuality and homosexuality, abnormalizing representations of same-sex desire simultaneously operate to legitimate heterosexuality and abnormalize same-sex desire (Sedgwick, 1990). I would suggest that an example of this process is the framing of queer youth in schools as "at risk" individuals whose sexuality is framed as their individual problem. This process reinforces notions of disease and deviance and simultaneously operates to normalize heterosexuality.

Cultural reproduction theories maintain that schools play a major role in reproducing the knowledge of dominant races, genders, classes, abilities, and sexualities. Within this framework heterosexuality can be seen as a form of cultural capital (Britzman, 1995; Quinlivan, 1996). Britzman suggested that the notion of sexual capital may help us to understand how sexual identities become normalized and also outlawed. This "political economy of sexualities" (Britzman, 1995, p. 69) can account for differences between the use and exchange values of heterosexuality and homosexuality in schools. So the use of deficit discourses to frame lesbian and gay sexuality at Riverside College can be seen as a way to contain and abnormalise same-sex desire without compromising the legitimization of hetero normative discourses within the school.

Apple (1995) suggested that schools are caught between two contradictory roles; the political role of ensuring equality and class mobility, and the economic role of producing agents for the labor market and the cultural capital of technical, administrative knowledge. In order to cope with that dilemma, schools recreated categories of deviance by stratifying students who could not contribute to the maximization of its production. Those students were labeled as "at risk" and consequently schools (within a North American context) became the recipients of relatively small amounts of state money to deal with the "problem."

Fine (1991) suggested that deficit discourses were a common way to contain low-income students and that the counseling arena in schools had become the commonest site within which social concerns have been constructed as personal and individual problems. She argued that in the process of marginalizing the interests of community and family, the hegemony of the dominant social class is preserved. Within this framework, schools can be seen to represent themselves as neutral, tending to reframe the "problem" as a private responsibility of the family as opposed to an issue which should be addressed within the (public) sphere of the school.

Drawing on these frameworks, the actions of constructing lesbian and gay students as "at risk" can be seen as a way for Riverside College to "have its cake and eat it too." The school can be seen to meet the needs of a disadvantaged group of individuals while at the same time surviving in the marketplace with its reputation intact and perhaps even enhanced. In the process, hetero normative discourses are reinforced while representations of same-sex desire are abnormalized.

"AT RISK" DISCOURSES AT THE MACRO LEVEL

Equity discourses aiming to provide some parity between groups within a pluralist society have been drawn on in the creation and use of the "at risk" label. Within the equity context, schools are seen as organizations which could effect some justice for disadvantaged groups (Middleton, 1988). The "at risk" model requires individual schools to identify disadvantaged students and provide strategies which will enable them to compete more equitably with other more "advantaged" students. Students who have been identified as "at risk" in a New Zealand context include girls, Maori and Pacific Island students, and truants (Education Review Office, 1997). Increasingly, the case is being made for adding lesbian, gay, and bisexual students to the list (Quinlivan, 1994; Town, 1996).

A substantial body of research (Khayatt, 1994; Mac An Ghaill, 1994; Quinlivan & Town, 1999; Trenchard & Warren, 1984) suggests that lesbian, gay, and bisexual students do experience significant barriers to learning. Their educational experiences have been characterized by high levels of verbal and physical harassment, feelings of isolation and depression, and being alone in their schools. As a result, they have a high level of truancy and often leave school at an earlier age without educational qualifications. In addition, the feelings of isolation experienced by queer youth may lead to feelings of low self-esteem and self-loathing (Quinlivan, 1996; Town, 1996). While overseas literature and research clearly establishes the need for lesbian, gay, and bisexual youth to be considered as an "at risk" group in terms of suicide attempts and ideation (Feinleib, 1989; Massachusetts State Education Department, 1995), it is only recently in a New Zealand context that the connections between lesbian and gay sexuality and the high rate of youth suicide have begun to be established (Ministry of Youth Affairs, 1997).

Researchers have also identified the ways in which current educational practices operate to produce representations that abnormalize and pathologize queer youth. Town (1996) discusses how framing gay male sexuality within HIV/AIDS discourses operates to reinforce notions of abnormality and (dis)ease. I have also drawn attention to the fact that due to the silences which surround representations of active female sexuality, and the overt headline grabbing physical violence that young gay men can be subjected to in schools, the perspectives of young lesbian women in schools are frequently silenced within the "at risk" equation (Quinlivan, 1996).

While there is no doubt that queer students in schools are "at risk," it is how this is translated into the school environment that is problematic. While Riverside College has not formally identified lesbian, gay, and bisexual students as an "at risk" group, I would suggest that drawing on the deficit model has enabled the school to frame those students' sexuality as a personal problem.

The New Zealand Ministry of Education has produced two documents that specify the legal responsibilities of schools in relation to meeting the needs of all students. The first of these is the National Education Guidelines (Ministry of Education, 1993), which contains three main goals for schools. The first of these goals indicates that it is the legal responsibility of all schools to ensure that programs should enable all youth to reach their full potential. The second goal is that equality of educational opportunity should be maintained by schools identifying and removing all barriers to achievement and success in their learning. The final legal obligation is that students with special needs should be identified and receive appropriate support.

In addition to the educational goals outlined in the previous document, National Administration Guidelines were also specified. These required the governing bodies of local schools, known as Boards of

Trustees, to provide a safe physical and emotional environment for students and to comply in full with any legislation currently in force or that may be developed to ensure the safety of students and employees (Education Review Office, 1997). The governmental organization, which ensures that individual schools meet their legal obligations, is known as the Education Review Office.

The Education Review Office has identified a number of school features that may contribute to an unsafe physical and emotional environment for students. While lesbian and gay students are not specifically identified as an at risk group, unsafe school practices which could be relevant to the issues facing lesbian and gay youth include sexual harassment, loneliness, and behavior of teachers and/or other students which induces fear (Education Review Office, 1997).

The Education Review Office points out that although the requirement to address barriers to learning is included in the mandatory guidelines for Boards of Trustees, there is no agreed definition of the term and no guidelines are provided for how schools are to overcome them (Education Review Office, 1997). In an attempt to provide some direction to schools in that respect, the Education Review Office recently suggested that in some schools a relevant and comprehensive health education program run in combination with an effective guidance network and clinical health services has gone some way to overcome these barriers to learning (Education Review Office, 1997). These three characteristics are all features of Riverside College.

The effect of the government legislation is to allow schools to only have to address issues for which there is an immediately identifiable and vocal representative group. In the case of lesbian, bisexual, and gay youth who often receive little parental support this may seem impossible or unnecessary. With the advent of neo-liberal educational reforms and the accompanying devolution of power to Boards of Trustees, it is up to individual school communities to choose whether to develop equity policies and procedures. The existence of equity policies, sexual harassment policies and procedures, and policies and procedures to protect students against bullying in schools is an indication that the school recognizes schools need to provide equitable environments for their students. However, the existence of these policies and procedures provides no guarantee that they will be acted on in order to protect the individual rights of students (Quinlivan, 1996).

WHAT DOES "AT RISK" MEAN IN TERMS OF EDUCATIONAL PRACTICE AT RIVERSIDE COLLEGE?

The notion of meeting the needs of individual students is one of the most prominent aims of the school as it is expressed in Riverside College's school charter. This sits well with the strong neo-liberal emphasis on individualism and individual responsibility, which is a strong ethos within the current devolutionary climate. Ball (1997) asserts that what has been achieved in the shift from welfare to workplace ethos is the creation of a new moral environment for both consumers and producers. The market celebrates the ethics of the "personal standpoint," the personal interests and desires of individuals. The emphasis on individual responsibility is a strong feature of "at risk" discourses which provide one form of equity in action in schools in the 1990s.

Within that context, any disadvantage is seen to be the responsibility of individual students, and support for them to come to terms with their personal problem is provided for them on a case by case basis through the guidance system. This framework of the "deficit model" can also provide a justification for schools to be seen to meet the needs of lesbian, gay, and bisexual students. While queer youth are being defined as "at risk" they can be classified as fitting within a deviant model which argues that they "need help." This solution neatly sidesteps the issue of "promotion" which could be leveled at schools who address issues of gay and lesbian sexuality and bisexuality (Silin, 1995). I would suggest that the school can claim to be addressing inclusion for lesbian and gay youth in a way that does not affect the marketability of their institution. It enables them to portray the school as an environment that endeavors to meet the needs of all students. It is not possible to move beyond addressing the needs of lesbian and gay students as a minority group of disadvantaged individuals in the school because it poses too much of a threat to the image of the school.

Richard, the gay male teacher, and Ryan, the gay senior student, whom I interviewed suggested that a school meeting the needs of lesbian, gay, and bisexual students could be perceived by the public as "promoting" and "recruiting for" queer sexuality. It is significant the power that nineteenth century constructions of deviance still have in the late twentieth century, especially in the private/public locus of schools where childhood is considered to be a time of sexual innocence (Silin, 1995). Participants noted that the pervasiveness of these discourses (Thonemann, 1999) did not sit easily with the requirements on schools to compete with each other in the current market-driven climate:

> [This school's] pretty gay friendly. Of course schools can't give that image . . . parents wouldn't send their kids here, a gay friendly school's a recruitment agency. People think like, gay people recruit. (Ryan, gay male student)

> There's an element in this school of the school being particularly sensitive to key families, parents, groups within the school community . . . the parents of the academic kids who hold more sway than the rest of the student body . . . and I think that . . . what the management is afraid of is that some of those key parents will find difficulty with what they see as promotion of lesbian and gay issues rather than spreading gay and lesbian issues through the curriculum. (Richard, gay male teacher)

The notion of schools as important sites of cultural reproduction is echoed in Richard's comments. He suggests that "key" (middle-class) parents may have some difficulty with the school advocating that lesbian and gay sexuality is just as normal as heterosexuality. Framing individual lesbian and gay students as having a personal problem, which the school works hard to address, is far less threatening than the idea that the school is "promoting" queer sexuality as normal. Who would argue with a philosophy which so clearly emphasizes nurturing and caring for individual students? As James, the school principal, pointed out to me:

> I think if a school was known as one that was supportive for gay and lesbian students and staff then I think that probably the community would draw the generalization that it was a caring school who tried to nurture all of the students and meet all their needs.

Constructing individual students as subjects of difference in compensatory discourses which frame differences within the deficit model also emerged in how students made sense of their gayness. When I asked Ryan, the gay male student, what was so good about Riverside College for him, he replied:

> Well the attitudes and the understanding, like someone said to me "You can't choose to be gay and if you ever want to talk" . . . (Ryan, gay male student)

Not being able to "choose" suggests a tolerance based on a "lack," the implication behind the person's response suggests that if you could choose then you would not be gay. Minoritizing discourses (Sedgwick, 1990) conceptualise queer students as a disadvantaged group in relation to the heterosexual norm. This sickness model leads back to nineteenth century constructions of homosexuals as diseased sexual deviants (Weeks, 1989). Within a deficit framework lesbian and gay students will always be "other," the marked (pathologized) half of the hetero/homo binary. Positioning lesbian and gay sexuality as a site of suffering serves to reinforce the normativity of heterosexuality and also reinforces the notion of sexuality as either a heterosexual or homosexual choice. The reinforcement of this binary privileges limited representations of sexuality over more diverse representations of sexuality. Bisexuality, for example, is rendered invisible. A deeper examination of the ways in which representations of gender and sexuality inform each other and are conflated in order to normalize heterosexuality is also avoided.

"At risk" discourses construct sexuality as private rather than political. The use of the "at risk" label then prevents schools from having to acknowledge that the actual problem lies within the culture of the school and in the way in which people and institutions actively produce normative constructions of (hetero) sexuality. This means that the school need go no further in attempting to meet the needs of lesbian and gay youth (Quinlivan, 1996; Sedgwick, 1990). As Richard, the gay male teacher, commented:

> [The school's] got a framework in place in terms of its policy to support lesbian and gay students but in fact there's nothing hanging on that structure, there are no official support structures for them, apart from the guidance counselor. (Richard, gay male teacher)

Suzanne, the lesbian teacher interviewed, felt that the current approach that the school was adopting did not go any way to challenging the homophobia which is such an endemic feature of students' lived culture in secondary schools (Mac An Ghaill, 1994; Quinlivan, 1996; Town, 1996):

> . . . all those sorts of (homophobic) comments that (some students) . . . make, would make some (lesbian and gay kids) feel a little bit hesitant about saying they really were. It is dealt with but it doesn't

> stop it . . . it's like putting out little fires rather than some sort of overall thing. (Suzanne, lesbian teacher)

Challenging the Deficit Model

Apple (1995) maintains that resistance, contestation, and lived culture make the work that schools perform as sites of ideological production complex and that it is important not to underestimate the resistance of teachers and students and the agency they exercise. Riverside College certainly reflects that complexity. It is important to acknowledge that, while the limitations of the school's primary approach to meeting the needs of lesbian and gay students is problematic, nevertheless Graeme the counselor, Richard, and Suzanne are all aware of the disadvantages of the model and attempt to do something to counteract it. The counselor is aware of the deficit model when dealing with lesbian and gay clients and attempts to work on reframing an understanding with students of where the "problem" of being lesbian and gay actually does lie and work with them to deal with homophobic attitudes:

> That (gay and lesbian) students see their sexuality as being a problem is obviously a concern. And with this particular boy that I've been seeing that was one of the issues we've worked on. He now accepts he doesn't have a problem, the problem now is other people, parents in particular. (Graeme, guidance counselor)

Richard, as an "out" gay teacher who has begun to work as an advocate in the school for lesbian and gay students, is also aware of the limitations of the deficit model and works to educate his colleagues and challenge their assumptions:

> . . . at this interview we had last week when the deputy principal said, "What are you going to do when you run up against other problems in the school?" to this (gay) kid . . . I had to say, "Well hang on a minute, what are we going to do with the other kids who have problems with Ryan being gay?" . . . those are the problems of the other kids in the school, they're not Ryan's problems. (Richard, gay male teacher)

In addition, the school has several other factors operating in its favor in terms of its ability to meet the needs of queer youth in the school. The presence of openly lesbian and gay teachers (Richard in particular) has played a particularly powerful role in educating and challenging heteronormative discourses in the school and acting as an advocate for gay youth (Thonemann, 1999). His work with colleagues has, perhaps most importantly, created a place for Ryan, as a gay male student, to feel safe and happy attending at Riverside College. Ryan explains:

> Well most of the teachers would be alright to talk about it and that. In Math today and my Math teacher, I didn't even know she knew said, "Oh have you read the book, *Am I Blue?*," and I said, "Oh yeah, I've read it" and she said, "I read it the other day and I thought it was very good." Most of the teachers here are gay-friendly. (Ryan, gay male student)

It is important to acknowledge that Riverside College has attempted to address the issues facing lesbian and gay youth in schools within a context where, up until recently, the issues facing queer youth in schools have been invisible and ignored. Perhaps attempting to meet the needs of students through identifying them as "at risk" individuals is all that is possible within the current educational climate where issues of social justice and equity take second place to notions of efficiency and competition (Gordon, 1994).

I would suggest that in our rush to establish lesbian, gay, and bisexual youth as an "at risk" group, as teachers and school administrators we need to think carefully about the way in which we unintentionally frame queer students as the problem, rather than considering that it is the heteronormative culture of schools which needs to be tackled. We need to think carefully about the extent to which lesbian, gay, and bisexual students are, in effect, re-pathologized, while normative constructions of heterosexuality remain unchallenged. Addressing the underlying culture of compulsory heterosexuality in schools is admittedly a more challenging and complex prospect. Becoming critically aware of the dangers which equity frameworks pose in constructing understandings of queer youth in schools may be helpful in this respect. It may also be useful for teachers and school administrators to consider ways in which schools can become environments where the complexities of sexual diversity beyond the narrow confines of lesbian and gay labels can be engaged with (Quinlivan, in press). This would perhaps enable understandings about sexual diversity to be widened, rather than limited and contained.

NOTE

1. All of the names of the participants and schools have been changed to protect their anonymity.

REFERENCES

Apple, M. (1995). *Education and power*. New York: Routledge.

Ball, S. (1997). Policy sociology and critical social research: A personal review of recent education policy and policy research. *British Educational Research Journal, 23*, 257-274.

Britzman, D. (1995). What is this thing called love? *Taboo: The Journal of Culture and Education, 1*, 65-91.

Education Review Office. (1997). *Students at risk: Barriers to learning, 7*. Wellington, New Zealand: Ministry of Education.

Epstein, D., & Johnson, R. (1998). *Schooling sexualities*. Buckingham: Open University Press.

Feinleib, M. (1989). *Report of the secretary's taskforce on youth suicide*. Washington: U.S. Department of Health and Human Services.

Fine, M. (1991). *Framing dropouts: Notes on the politics of an urban high school*. New York: State University of New York Press.

Gordon, L. (1994). Whatever happened to the national policy for the education of girls and women in New Zealand? *New Zealand Women's Studies Journal, 10*, 35-45.

Khayatt, D. (1994). Surviving school as a lesbian student. *Gender & Education, 6*, 47-59.

Luke, L., & Gore, C. (1992). *Feminisms and critical pedagogy*. New York: Routledge.

Mac An Ghaill, M. (1994). (In)visibility: Sexuality, race and masculinity in the school context. In D. Epstein (Ed.), *Challenging lesbian and gay inequalities in education* (pp. 152-176) Bristol: Open University Press.

Massachusetts State Education Department. (1995). *Youth risk behavior study*. Boston, Massachusetts: Author.

Middleton, S. (1988). Women, equality and equity in liberal educational policies 1945-1988: A feminist critique. In J. Codd (Ed.), *New Zealand educational policy today* (pp. 68-93). Palmerston North: Dunmore Press.

Ministry of Education. (1993). *National education guidelines*. Wellington, New Zealand: Author.

Ministry of Youth Affairs. (1997). *An approach for action: Phase two in the development of a national strategy to help prevent youth suicide in New Zealand*. Wellington, New Zealand: Ministry of Health.

Quinlivan, K. (in press). "On Dangerous Ground": What's possible in terms of affirming sexual diversity in schools in the 1990s? Unpublished doctoral thesis, University of Canterbury, Christchurch, New Zealand.

Quinlivan, K. (1996). "Claiming an identity they taught me to despise": Lesbian students respond to the regulation of same sex desire. *New Zealand Women's Studies Journal 12*(2), 99-113.

Quinlivan, K., & Town, S. (1999). Queer as fuck? Exploring the potential of queer pedagogies in researching school experiences of lesbian and gay youth. In D. Epstein & J. Sears (Eds.), *A dangerous knowing: Sexuality, pedagogy and popular culture* (pp. 242-256). London: Cassell.

Sedgwick, E. (1990). *Epistemology of the closet*. Los Angeles: University of California Press.

Silin, J. (1995). *Sex, death and education: Our passion for ignorance in the age of AIDS*. New York: Teachers College Press.

Thonemann, A. (1999). *Enabling and disabling conditions for teaching against homophobia*. Paper presented at the New Zealand and Australian Association for Research in Education conference, Melbourne, Australia.

Town, S. (1996). *Is it safe to come out yet? The impact of secondary schooling on the positive identity development of ten young gay men*. Paper presented at the American Education Research Association conference, New York.

Trenchard, L., & Warren, H. (1984). *Something to tell you*. London: London Gay Teenage Group.

Weeks, J. (1989). *Sex, politics and society: The regulation of sexuality since 1800*. London: Longman.

Banking Goodwill: Working Towards Children's Happiness and Safety at School Through the Strategies We've Learnt as Lesbian Mothers–A Personal Reflection

Teresa Savage

SUMMARY. Drawing on the experience of three children's education in seven schools across two hemispheres, Teresa Savage reflects on what she has learned about schools and education as a lesbian mother. She discusses the range of her children's responses to school, from the crying, painfully shy four-year-old son, to the aplomb of her seventeen-year-old daughter when organizing a school float for the Sydney Gay and Lesbian Mardi Gras. The effectiveness of teachers in defending her children from homophobic prejudice is explored, as well as the impact of dominant school cultures on lesbian mothers. Teresa Savage explains that, with her partner, she has developed a simple balance sheet for interaction with schools, banking goodwill through volunteering and participation, while offering constructive criticism and, sometimes, forthright anger. In her experience, this has been the best way to maximize her children's happiness, safety, and achievement. *[Article copies available for a fee from The Haworth Document Delivery Service: 1-800-HAWORTH. E-mail address: <getinfo@haworthpressinc.com> Website: <http://www.HaworthPress.com> © 2002 by The Haworth Press, Inc. All rights reserved.]*

Teresa Savage, MA, Writing (UTS), BSc, Dip. Lib., works as a librarian in public health.

[Haworth co-indexing entry note]: "Banking Goodwill: Working Towards Children's Happiness and Safety at School Through the Strategies We've Learnt as Lesbian Mothers–A Personal Reflection." Savage, Teresa. Co-published simultaneously in *Journal of Gay & Lesbian Social Services* (Harrington Park Press, an imprint of The Haworth Press, Inc.) Vol. 14, No. 2, 2002, pp. 33-42; and: *From Here to Diversity: The Social Impact of Lesbian and Gay Issues in Education in Australia and New Zealand* (ed: Kerry H. Robinson, Jude Irwin, and Tania Ferfolja) Harrington Park Press, an imprint of The Haworth Press, Inc., 2002, pp. 33-42. Single or multiple copies of this article are available for a fee from The Haworth Document Delivery Service [1-800-HAWORTH, 9:00 a.m. - 5:00 p.m. (EST). E-mail address: getinfo@haworthpressinc.com].

KEYWORDS. Lesbian mothers, schooling, education, homophobia, prejudice, children, safety

It's early evening at our place. I fly in the front door, trip over the dog, throw down my bag, and yell out "Hi" to the kids. "Ho" comes back to me from a cluttered bedroom. "What are you doing?" "Math homework." "Have you fed the kittens? Done your cello practice? Emptied your lunchbox?" As I yell, I flick the red button on the phone that replays the messages. What I hear makes me smile. It's a message for my partner, and it goes like this; "Louise, it's Jeanette here from the school canteen. You'll never believe it, but I've had someone ring me and volunteer to help with canteen on Friday. So guess what? You can have the day off. Have a good day!" Louise will be so pleased. She's been juggling her heavy workload to volunteer at the school canteen every fourth Friday for the past six years.

* * *

My partner, Louise, and I have three children, all born within our relationship. We seem to have been dealing with schooling issues for an eternity, but I suppose it's about seventeen years. Our son Rowan is twenty years old and in third year university. Maeve is seventeen and currently tackling the horrendous final year Higher School Certificate, while Grainne is in those directionless middle high school years, not quite a young woman, but not a child either. We have always been equal parents to all three children, and have taken equal responsibility for them.

Being a lesbian mother and dealing with schools as institutions is a tricky balancing act. While we have found that a degree of normalizing, on our part, allows our children to get the best out of the system with the least harm, neither of us would want that to be seen as an excuse for an educational system which still works within a societally dominant framework. Heterosexual family norms, notwithstanding domestic violence, incest, and neglect, are maintained within the school system and continually upheld as the ideal environment for raising children. The converse of this, broadly speaking, portrays lesbian families as a poor substitute. And our children, without careful and untiring support from us, can so easily absorb that message.

We are ambitious for our children. We've always wanted them to do well at school. To be absolutely honest, we've wanted them to excel. We've devoted vast amounts of time to helping them with homework.

We've also listened to music practice, taught them to cook, how to use the library and the computer, how to drive, play cards and board games and charades, read thousands of books to them, played soccer and surfed and danced, gone to movies and art galleries and operas and plays and museums, traveled widely, cuddled up in bed on cold or sad nights, shopped endlessly for that elusive something, debated and argued and considered. In short, we've been very involved parents, and have loved it. But there's no doubt that we've had a mighty drive to encourage the highest achievement possible for them. Where does this come from? Perhaps a feeling in both of us that we could have done better ourselves, that our career paths haven't quite presented us with enough intellectual content, that our own parents were too busy or too self-absorbed or too alienated to give us the encouragement we needed. I don't think that is particular to lesbian mothers–as many lesbian mothers would eschew parental ambition as embrace it. But it's always been very important to Louise and me that our children do as well as they possibly can in any subject or activity. I mention this to lend caution to any impression that we've found a blueprint for dealing with the education system. Lesbian mothers do not have one unifying set of interests. How we deal with school depends on a wide variety of factors and viewpoints. Some want academic excellence, some want education without competition, some want single sex not co-educational, some want lots of sport or music. What we all want is for our children to be cherished and encouraged.

What Louise and I have learnt about school, over the years, is that for children to succeed there, and be happy, parents have to be involved. For the children of lesbian mothers, there is a disparity, a mismatch, a deep separation between the world of school and their home environments. Values are different. Norms clash. Drawing defining pictures of your family in kindergarten, right through to sex education in high school–the daily need to explain or exert difference–must be a strain on children and young people. For parents, being involved with the schooling process at any level smooths the dissonance, bridges the gaps, allows the edges of those two competing worlds to overlap a little.

Louise and I have worked in our children's schools in many capacities. We both believe in the idea of building social capital in communities, and see involvement with schools as an excellent way of creating a more equitable and caring society. In our children's primary school, Louise organized and set off the fireworks display for cracker night every year for nine years, while I was known as the vegieburger queen, setting up a barbecue to cater for the vegetarians at every major school event. In the early years, we both went into the classroom to listen to children read and to help them learn computer and research skills. I've volunteered in the school library, covering books and tidying shelves in a sort of busperson's holiday from my own job as a librarian. We've both been members of panels, and carted furniture around for school plays. I've been to gardening days and collected money for allowing cars to be parked in school grounds. Louise has been a volunteer in the school canteen for six years. Strangely, most of this volunteering has been a pleasure, rather than a chore.

Neither of us has ever chosen to be involved with a school committee. School committees are essential for initiating and maintaining those activities that enrich the learning experience of our children. Parents who work on the performing arts committees, the soccer and netball support groups, and the debating committees contribute significantly to a notion of education that is much broader than the academic. But, in our experience, school committees regularly degenerate into power struggles between parent factions, and gripe sessions against teachers. Neither of us has ever had the stomach for sitting through endless discussions of standards of school uniform or whether the school canteen should sell Mars bars. I know many good hearted people who have tried to bring a sense of reason to it all, working incredibly hard to generate an open, positive atmosphere. I admire those brave souls immensely. But somehow, the need for some members of the school community to exercise their egos in the school forum is intense. But perhaps I am too cynical. It could be that I can't bear going to school committees because they are too much like the frustrating bureaucratic meetings I attend daily at work. Whatever the reason, I acknowledge that I don't have the patience. I'd rather be pulling weeds out of the playground flowerbeds, or serving the tea at the school musicale.

Our first experience of school, in England in the early eighties, was not good. After one year in the nursery class, Rowan received a report from the teacher that said that he was very shy, and she had grave fears for his future because of his family background. We were outraged. In England, at least at that time, educational reports remained on your school record through the whole of your education, following you from primary to high school. I could not allow a teacher's prejudice to follow Rowan around. Speaking directly with the teacher proved fruitless, so I went to the school principal. She was in a difficult position. But after listening patiently, she simply shrugged her shoulders and commented to me that it was strange how often documents get lost in the system (indicating her willingness to make the report "disappear"). The teacher was not challenged, but Rowan was not labeled.

Rowan was painfully shy and very young (four years and three weeks) when he started full-time school. He cried every morning for three years when we left him. A friend of his, a very strong little girl, told us one day that Rowan spent every playtime staring down a drain. Luckily, Rowan was blessed with a wonderful teacher, who simply accepted his shyness and kept him on her lap for the first half-hour of every day. He remained in a vertically grouped class for three years, with this same teacher, and developed into a very confident and competent class member, with a loving and very diverse group of friends. This teacher had a gift for recognizing the strengths in all her little charges, in fostering cooperation and acceptance in all activities, and in seeing the funny side of teaching. In one of her reports about Rowan, which I still have, she wrote, "In art work Rowan has a very positive relationship with Sellotape."

But we did have to think about the issues thrown up by this first encounter with the state school system. Was Rowan's shyness connected to us and our relationship? The temptation, particularly with a first child, to blame any problems on our status as lesbian mothers was always there. But I don't think so. Classrooms, busting at the seams with thirty energetic little bodies, are very unreal social settings. Perhaps open plan offices come close to it in our adult lives, but school teaches socialization within a structure that is rare in adulthood. Surviving in a classroom is not preparation for surviving in the workplace, or any other adult scenario. Rowan has always found large groups with competing noise and activity difficult. He has always been a quiet person who prefers his own company (or, in reality, the company of books) to being with a crowd. Perhaps he was just innately shy, but it could be that when I was at home with him when he was little I was very inexperienced. I had no idea what you do with babies. It never occurred to me that it might be a good idea to socialize with other children. I thought that if we were at home, we might as well do what I'd always liked doing, so I read to him, and talked with him, and listened to music. A friend who looked after him when he was two years old read him the complete Greek myths and legends, and he loved it, never fidgeting or interrupting, just taking it all in. We will always be grateful to Rowan's infants' teacher for never ever suggesting that Rowan had any serious problem. For always reassuring us that he would be fine. For always having confidence in us as parents. For talking often with us. For being patient, and bringing out the best qualities in a shy little boy who preferred to live in his imagination rather than tackle the rough and tumble of the playground.

And what of teachers generally? The vast majority of teachers we've been involved with have a great deal of goodwill, are strongly committed to the education and welfare of children, and are glad for any child who has two concerned and loving parents. Many teachers have freely and generously given their time to my children outside normal school hours, in a way that most of us are never expected to in our working lives. They appreciate loving families above all, for loving families produce happy and willing learners. But, like all of us, they find it hard to adapt to criticism, particularly if that is the sum total of feedback they receive.

For criticism to be accepted and acted upon, it has to be positive. We soon found that only contacting the school when we had a complaint rarely resulted in a resolution of the problem. Teachers, already overstretched, would react resentfully to mothers who only ever contacted them to whinge. Giving regular positive feedback to teachers, both verbally and in writing, goes a long way to ensuring that when you do have a complaint, it will be seriously considered.

So, how is it that being involved in working bees and clean-up days contributes to children's happiness and safety at school? Firstly, by simply going into schools and working alongside other parents and teachers, you become familiar with the culture of the school. Once, when I was digging out a flowerbed at Maeve's large, highly prestigious, academically selective high school, on a weekend working bee, I started groaning about tough roots and bloody invasive plants to the person next to me. She murmured agreement. When I looked up I realized that I was working alongside the school principal, who was happily tugging away at lantana roots. As I smiled and focused back on my task, I realized that she was wearing odd gym shoes, both white but with very different stitch patterns. "Couldn't find a pair," she laughed. There was something sweetly human about that incident. Neither in my mind, nor hers, could formality or hierarchy divide us ever again. And over the years, in engaging with the inevitable teenage railing against school uniform, late note policy, school sport, and bus etiquette, I could keep that principal's mismatched shoes in mind, and it allowed me to consider, rather than condemn, her viewpoint.

Conversely, and as much as I hate this idea, there is nothing more humanizing across race, class, and culture than sweating together over a white hot barbecue plate, serving vegieburgers to the starving hordes. Homophobia depends on sweeping generalizations. Regular, ordinary contact with individual lesbians gradually undermines that prejudice. The more straight teachers and parents pass us buttered rolls to fill, or laugh over a glass of wine at the end of a long summer fete, the more three dimensional we become. Lesbian mothers cannot be demonized or stereotyped if we are seen in our ordinary, everyday capacity, with our ordinary, everyday concerns. If we are perceived as fully rounded people, our concerns will be taken seriously.

I'm not arguing for a forced involvement here. I can honestly say that I've loved the small revelations that come with working alongside people of very different racial and class backgrounds. Shared hard work is a great leveler. I've had great fun with parents and teachers who I would never mix with otherwise. And I'm proud that our children are being brought up within school environments where racial difference, in particular, is totally normal.

Of course, no positive outcome can be gained from visibility as a lesbian mother in the school community without coming out. We always do, regularly and tediously, explain our family to fellow volunteers, children, and teachers. Louise says she's often tempted to just tell them she's a single parent whose husband got run over by a bus. "Why should I have to tell them my life story?" she grumbles. "They don't have to tell me theirs." But she inevitably, patiently, and with a generous smile, explains that I am her partner, that our children have two mothers, and that's the way it's always been for them. We both regularly resist the implications of biology–but who gave birth to them?–and have to assert our rights as equal parents. We rigidly cross out sections on school forms which ask for father, and add another column for mother. One particularly difficult primary principal became aware that Louise gave birth to Maeve, and would pointedly only speak to Louise about her progress. We objected, and then made a huge effort to only deal with that principal together. Most teachers are only too pleased to speak with either of us about our children.

To look at it the other way, however, we've needed to consider how our involvement affects the school. When I visited Rowan's all male academically selective high school I was often overwhelmed by the stink of testosterone. It was all in my nostrils, of course. But I held on to the feeling that simply by walking along the corridors, wandering into the library, sauntering across the rowdy playground, I changed the chemical mix of that school. Female presence, and yes, lesbian presence, had to have some impact. Being there showed a willingness to engage with what often felt like the enemy. It was important for Rowan to see that we were prepared to take it on, to see what it was like to try to survive in that environment, to make small challenges to the antiquated patriarchal hierarchy of an all-boys state school which aspired to be a private one. When we came home after a stint of helping park cars in the school grounds to raise money, or ferrying the debating team around, we knew what he faced every day. We knew what an onslaught he endured.

In our experience, school for the child of lesbian mothers is very different for boys and for girls. Quite frankly, the vast majority of girls and their parents don't give a hoot. They couldn't care less if our girls have two mums. Neither do the teachers at their girls-only high schools. I've raked through my memory of Grainne's experience of school, but I can't recall one single experience where a teacher's reaction to her lesbian family has adversely affected her schooling. It's just not been an issue.

But perhaps the difference for our children has been in the enormous changes that have occurred in relation to visibility for lesbians over our period of mothering. When I tell my children that I was once refused a job because I am a lesbian, or that the first women's group I was in had a discussion and vote on whether I, as a lesbian, should be allowed to be a member, they stare in disbelief. Over twenty years, in our lives at least, things have changed. Rowan started school at a time when lesbian-chic was not even a twinkle in the eye, when public careers were ruined at the sniff of a girlie involvement, when blatant discrimination in employment and housing were commonplace. Things changed fast, but Rowan's early education was with a background of more overt hostility to lesbian lifestyle and choices.

Historical realities notwithstanding, the real reason for the troubles Rowan faced at school lie in the perceived dangers of lesbians bringing up boys. Over the years, Louise and I have faced inordinately more well-meaning concern in bringing up a boy than in bringing up the girls. People worry about boys. Boys are seen as on the one hand more brash and insensitive, and on the other more fragile than girls. Boys are insecure, and their developing manhood can be so easily warped by the wrong influences. Other parents, work colleagues, and even friends have seen it as perfectly reasonable to throw out the challenge at regular intervals through Rowan's life–don't you think he needs a male role model? Enraged, I'd respond facetiously–show me one that's worth having, and I'll give it a go! In reality, Rowan is part of a large extended family with the usual number and variety of male relatives. He's had many male teachers. He was very fond of the old man who lived next door. I once asked Rowan about this issue, when he was seven or eight years old. "Do you think you've missed out, not having a dad?" I asked him, terrified that I was planting the seed for an insecurity that didn't currently exist. "Nah," he said, glancing up from his book, "most of my friends' dads just chugalug beer and change the telly channel over to sport without asking."

But Rowan faced a great deal of harassment at school. In the early part of high school he was targeted as gay by association, and suffered all the ramifications of homophobia. Boys taunted him, opened his school bag and emptied cans of Coke into it, tugged at his clothes until they were torn, hit and pushed and tripped him. The son of another lesbian at his school told his mother that she could never come out there, because of what happened to Rowan. On one occasion, a boy hit him so hard across the back with a fencing foil (we'd innocently thought fencing might be a good alternative to rugby!) that I took photographs of the welt when he arrived home from school, and took him straight to see a doctor. The next morning I went to see Rowan's year advisor, a man sporting a garishly checked blazer, pink bow tie, and matching pink socks, and was told that my son was very eccentric, so this kind of thing was only to be expected. When I insisted on speaking with the school principal, I was told that boys of this age are notoriously "Neanderthal." I was a screaming harpy. Deeply, deeply, I wanted to do terrible things to them. Prize off their fingernails perhaps, or hang them from the school flagpole. It's hard to explain the protectiveness of mothering. Poor Rowan had to stick it out the best he could, having a daily struggle with the pack mentality of early adolescent boys en masse. We contacted other schools, but with his usual quiet inner strength, in stark contrast to the demeanor of boys and teachers alike, Rowan insisted on claiming his place at that school. He endured it all with incredible resilience. Thankfully, the last couple of years he was there saw a definite change in his peers, and suddenly difference was original and cool. In years eleven and twelve Rowan was admired for his intellect, creativity, and unconventional approach. But his happiness had come at an unreasonable cost.

Maeve has a very different furrow to plough. Being at an academically selective high school in the inner city, she has grown through her teenage years with a group of friends whose parents are inner-city left wing academics and public servants. Amongst them are a progressive high court judge, an international expert on gender and education, and several long-term feminists. Perhaps Maeve chose these friends for the very reason that she knew she would be accepted. Whatever the reason, it has proved to be a supportive, though often turbulent, group. Last year, Maeve and one of her friends decided they would like to have a float from their school in the Sydney Gay and Lesbian Mardi Gras. It is a mark of the positive nature of her school that she even thought such a thing possible. We were full of pride for our girl as she negotiated with students, the school principal, other parents, and old girls. The principal, left unsupported by the education department, advised against the idea. Maeve raged against homophobia and the denial of free speech, and regretted the principal's lack of courage. But she always kept in mind that her school should be the last school publicly accused of prejudice. When the press got a sniff of the story, she was desperate to save her school from unjust criticism, and with the help of an experienced aunt, wrote a press release that explained their concerns but did not damage the school. She and her friends revamped their float to be called "Censored in High School" and forty of them had a great night raucously representing the needs of the younger generation of lesbian and bisexual school students.

As parents we were happy to stand beside Maeve, watching over her as she dealt so well with many competing interests and viewpoints. She learnt so much through this incident. (Will she have a future as a political lobbyist?) But I did send a letter to her school principal. In it I noted that for the principal to state publicly that the school supports equal rights for young lesbians, and gay and lesbian people in general, would be a significant landmark in protecting students from discrimination, violence, and self-destructive behaviors. History shows that the capacity of an influential individual to 'stick their neck out' is often the catalyst for change, particularly in the area of discrimination. We are hoping that next year, the principal will be able to take that step and march with girls, teachers, and parents under a banner that says 'Our High School supports the lesbian and gay community.'

One more thing, too. Our children are all vegetarians. That's fully vegetarian–"no chicken, no fish, thank you "–as I'm compelled to write on school excursion notes. It may be hard for meat-eating dykes to appreciate, but being a vegetarian child is often as defining a characteristic as being the child of lesbians. Our children have returned from school camps having not eaten anything but apples and carrots for days. They've been urged by parents of school friends, and teachers, to just try a little chicken or fish. They've been subjected to flip predictions that they'll never be able to resist McDonald's when they are teenagers. Difference is not always tolerated or respected. Our children have to explain themselves in more ways than one. And they remain committed, even sometimes scarily evangelical, vegetarians.

This is what we've done to protect our children through their school years. It may not work for everyone, but it could be worth trying for other lesbian mothers who find themselves at odds with schools and teachers. Louise will continue to volunteer at the school canteen until Maeve finishes her final year. I'll keep toting my gardening gloves and trowel to clean-up days. For us, it's been the best way to ensure Rowan, Maeve, and Grainne's happiness and success. And I haven't even mentioned the ultimate sacrifice that Louise makes. Ever wondered what it feels like to be a vegetarian serving hot meat pies?

Why Queer Theory Is Useful in Teaching: A Perspective from English as a Second Language Teaching

Cynthia D. Nelson

SUMMARY. In education there has been growing interest in making teaching practices more inclusive of lesbian, gay, and bisexual people and issues. However, the emphasis on including–and legitimating–"subordinate" sexual identities is being challenged by queer theory, which draws on post-structuralist theories of identity. With queer theory, the aim is not to accomplish inclusion but to facilitate inquiry–that is, to investigate the ways in which sexual identities are negotiated through day to day social interactions. This paper draws on literature from queer theory and English language teaching in order to explain why queer theory may be useful when serving groups who are culturally and/or linguistically heterogeneous. *[Article copies available for a fee from The Haworth Document Delivery Service: 1-800-HAWORTH. E-mail address: <getinfo@haworthpressinc.com> Website: <http://www.HaworthPress.com> © 2002 by The Haworth Press, Inc. All rights reserved.]*

Cynthia D. Nelson, PhD, MATESL, BA, is affiliated with the English Language Study Skills Assistance Centre, Faculty of Humanities and Social Sciences, University of Technology, Sydney.

Address correspondence to: ELSSA Centre, University of Technology, Sydney, PO Box 123, Broadway NSW 2007, Australia (E-mail: cynthia.nelson@uts.edu.au).

Author note: For offering critical feedback during the writing of this paper I thank Fran Byrnes, Chris Candlin, Francesca Guimaraens and Carolyn Williams. For providing some material support I thank Macquarie University for an Australian Postgraduate Award and the English Language Study Skills Assistance Centre of the University of Technology, Sydney, under the direction of Alex Barthel.

[Haworth co-indexing entry note]: "Why Queer Theory Is Useful in Teaching: A Perspective from English as a Second Language Teaching." Nelson, Cynthia D. Co-published simultaneously in *Journal of Gay & Lesbian Social Services* (Harrington Park Press, an imprint of The Haworth Press, Inc.) Vol. 14, No. 2, 2002, pp. 43-53; and: *From Here to Diversity: The Social Impact of Lesbian and Gay Issues in Education in Australia and New Zealand* (ed: Kerry H. Robinson, Jude Irwin, and Tania Ferfolja) Harrington Park Press, an imprint of The Haworth Press, Inc., 2002, pp. 43-53. Single or multiple copies of this article are available for a fee from The Haworth Document Delivery Service [1-800-HAWORTH, 9:00 a.m. - 5:00 p.m. (EST). E-mail address: getinfo@haworthpressinc.com].

KEYWORDS. Queer theory, gay and lesbian, education, English as a Second Language (ESL), cultural diversity, sexual identities

INTRODUCTION

In the field of education there has been increasing interest in making classrooms and curricula more inclusive and affirmative of gay, lesbian, and bisexual people and issues. This interest has been evident across a range of educational areas and levels, including secondary level English, social studies, and sexuality studies (e.g., Harris, 1990; Hart, 1989; edited volumes such as Epstein, 1994; Laskey & Beavis, 1996; Sears, 1992), tertiary level composition (e.g., Malinowitz, 1995; Parmeter & Reti, 1988), women's studies (e.g., Garber, 1994) and of course lesbian/gay/queer studies (e.g., Phillips, 1996). Similar efforts to make learning environments more "gay-friendly" have also been occurring within English language teaching (e.g., Hirst, 1981; Nelson, 1993a; Snelbecker, 1994; Summerhawk, 1998; see also Kato, 1999 on lesbian/gay international students). This paper emerges from my recent PhD research on teaching lesbian/gay content in English as a Second Language (ESL) classes (Nelson, 1999, 2000).

An ESL perspective on lesbian/gay/bisexual issues in education may be useful to educators, trainers, social service practitioners, and others who are not themselves language teachers. This is because many groups, not just ESL classes, are international, intercultural, and linguistically diverse. Also, the focus on communication and culture that typifies ESL classes is of central importance across a range of educational contexts. Therefore, those whose work involves dealing with lesbian/gay issues that arise within linguistically and culturally diverse groups may have an interest in how such issues are being approached in ESL. Ways of theorizing sexual identities may also be of interest to teachers and practitioners because the theories that underpin teaching practices are an important aspect of those practices. The central argument of this paper is that queer theory offers a flexible, open-ended framework for addressing lesbian/gay issues within linguistically and culturally diverse groups.

This paper:

- outlines key concerns in making learning/teaching environments more "gay-friendly."

- describes the origins of queer theory and the meanings of the term "queer."
- explains how a queer theory framework differs from a lesbian/gay identity framework and why queer theory may be of use educationally.

CREATING GAY-FRIENDLY ENVIRONMENTS FOR TEACHING AND LEARNING

In ESL journals, newsletters, and conference presentations, it has been argued that there is a need to make teaching practices and learning environments more gay-friendly. This involves:

- addressing heterosexist discrimination at educational institutions and homophobic attitudes among teachers, administrators, and students (Anderson, 1997; Brems & Strauss, 1995; Hirst, 1981; Nelson, 1993a).
- making curricula, resources and teaching practices more gay-inclusive (e.g., Carscadden, Nelson & Ward, 1992; Hanson, 1998; Jones & Jack, 1994; in English as a Foreign Language see Neff, 1992; Summerhawk, 1998), for example, by integrating the topic of lesbian and gay relationships within discussions of families, or homophobia within discussions of social discrimination.
- considering the educational needs of learners who themselves identify as lesbian, bisexual, or gay (Kappra, 1998/1999; Nelson, 1993a) and those who encounter gay people or issues in their everyday lives.
- creating learning and working environments where any learner or teacher (not just straight ones) can be open about their sexual identity without fear of reprisals (Censotti, 1998; Destandau, Nelson & Snelbecker, 1995; Mittler & Blumenthal, 1994; Nelson, 1993a; Saint Pierre, 1994; Shore, 1992; Snelbecker, 1994).
- mobilizing support within the profession–for example, Teachers of English to Speakers of Other Languages (TESOL), an international organization, established a task force (now a caucus) to investigate lesbian, gay, and bisexual concerns in relation to policy and pedagogy (see Cummings & Nelson, 1993a; Nelson, 1993b).

Much of the work cited above, along with similar work in other educational areas, seeks to make existing curricula (or policies) more inclusive by adding representations of subordinate sexual identities. The (often unstated) aim is to promote what Britzman (1995, p. 158) calls "pedagogies of inclusion." The theoretical framework underlying this gay-inclusive approach is a lesbian/gay identity framework. However, over the past decade this theoretical framework has been challenged by queer theory, an emerging body of work which draws on poststructuralist theories of identity (e.g., Butler, 1990; Fuss, 1991; Sedgwick, 1990; for descriptive historical accounts see Seidman, 1993, 1995). In recent years educators have begun to consider the educational implications of queer theory (in ESL see Nelson, 1999, 2000; in education see Britzman, 1995; Sumara & Davis, 1999; in tertiary education see Fuss, 1991; Malinowitz, 1995; Phillips, 1996). In order to consider the key concepts of queer theory and what they might offer teachers and social service practitioners, it is important to understand why queer theory originated.

WHY QUEER THEORY ORIGINATED

In response to the widespread invisibility and pathologizing of "homosexuals," the gay liberation movement of the 1960s and the subsequent creation of a lesbian and gay community and culture encouraged an out-and-proud approach (Seidman, 1995, writing of the United States). What made it possible to form a cohesive social movement based on gayness was the notion that gay or lesbian identity expressed an inner, universal essence (essentialism). During the 1970s and '80s, growing recognition that gay or lesbian identity was not innate but socially constructed (social constructivism) did not significantly change the widespread belief that gayness was a "fact" that could be either acknowledged or denied, expressed (albeit in culturally determined ways) or suppressed (for detailed accounts of this period see Seidman, 1993, 1995).

As the gay/lesbian movement and community gained visibility and political clout, the focus began to shift from what its "members" had in common to what they did not. Gathered together under the political/cultural umbrella of a gay movement were people who identified as lesbian, gay, bisexual, and transgendered. Their sexual practices, sexual values, relationship styles, multiple identities, and political affiliations were not only diverse but in some cases conflicting. Meanwhile, critical theorists and linguists were theorizing identities not as socially constructed *facts* but as cultural and discursive *acts* (e.g., Gumperz & Cook-Gumperz, 1982; LePage & Tabouret-Keller, 1985).

As a result of practical and theoretical challenges to identity-based social movements, in the mid-1980s queer theory and activism were developed. Whereas sexual identity formed the very basis of the lesbian/gay movement and community, queer theory makes sexual identity the subject of critique. The word "queer" is used to encompass "lesbian," "gay," "bisexual," and "transgender," but "queer" is also used to challenge clear-cut notions of sexual identity, purposely blurring the boundaries between identity categories (Warner, 1993). The paradoxical tension between the two meanings of queer–on the one hand including all "minority" sexual identities and on the other protesting the very notion of sexual identity–is central to queer theory.

WHY QUEER THEORY IS USEFUL IN TEACHING

Theorizing Sexual Identities as Acts Rather than Facts

According to queer theory, gay identity is not discovered and then expressed, but is actually produced through repeated discursive acts. In other words, sexual identities are not descriptive but performative–not what people *are* but what they *do* (Butler, 1990, drawing on Austin's [1962] notion of linguistic performativity). In this view, sexual identities are not personal attributes or individual constructions but culturally readable acts that are being created or "performed" during social interactions.

From a teaching or training perspective, there are several advantages to theorizing sexual identities as culturally readable acts rather than inner, universal essences. For one, this situates sexual identities within the realm of the ordinary–negotiating day-to-day interactions routinely involves "performing" and interpreting sexual identities. Secondly, it keeps the focus on observable behavior–what people say and do rather than who they feel they are. This is useful in those teaching contexts (such as ESL) where a major objective is to demystify social interactions unfamiliar to those who are new to, or outside of, a particular culture or subculture. With queer theory, it becomes possible to examine the linguistic and cultural patterns through which sexual identities are communicated, even constituted. Finally, the notion of "performativity" makes it clear that sexual identities are not universally accomplished but may be produced or "read" in different ways in different cultural contexts (see Livia & Hall, 1997). Acknowledging this diversity, and being able to examine it, are crucial to achieving intercultural understanding.

Problematizing All Sexual Identities Rather than Legitimizing Subordinate Ones

Lesbian/gay activism has sought to ensure that people who do not identify as heterosexual are not denied the same rights and privileges that are automatically accorded to those who do identify as heterosexual. Implicit to such efforts is the notion that it is possible, even desirable, to categorize people according to sexual identities. But queer theorists caution that sexual identities can be limiting as well as liberating, for they rely on exclusion as well as inclusion (Butler, 1991; Fuss, 1991; see also Foucault, 1990). In this view, affirming subordinate sexual identities has the (unintended) effect of reinforcing a hierarchical system, one that insists on solidifying sexualities into sexual identities, which can then be divided into those that are considered socially "acceptable" and those that are not. Rather than affirming sexual identity categories, queer theory questions the need for them. Rather than legitimizing minority sexual identities, queer theory problematizes *all* sexual identities.

In terms of teaching and learning, problematizing sexual identities does not mean presenting them in negative ways. On the contrary, it makes it possible to explore how acts of identity are not necessarily straightforward or transparent but can be complex, changing, and contested. It also acknowledges that, for a myriad of reasons, not everyone relates to a clear-cut identity category. To put it another way, acknowledging that identities are not truths, facts or things, but theoretical constructs that "arise at specific times, in specific places, to do specific work" (Poynton, 1997, p. 17) does not dismiss the need for identities nor their limitations. Instead, this approach makes it possible to ask what purpose identities serve, how they work, and also what constraints, dilemmas, or contradictions may be associated with them. In the end, problematizing all sexual identities may actually be more "inclusive" than simply validating subordinate sexual identities, because it allows for a wider range of experiences and perspectives to be considered. It may also be more practicable, since teachers or trainers are not expected to transmit knowledge (which they may or may not have) but to frame tasks that encourage investigation and inquiry.

Considering Sexual Identities Potentially Significant to Anyone

Queer theorists discuss a "heterosexual/homosexual binary" by which sexual identities are defined. The argument is that questions of definition are meaningful not just to "a small, distinct, relatively fixed homosexual minority" ("a minoritizing view") but to "people across the spectrum of sexualities" ("a universalizing view") (Sedgwick, 1990, p. 1). One reason for this is that the hetero/homosexual binary shapes the production of all sexual identities–not just gay ones. That is, "heterosexuality" has meaning only in relation to "homosexuality," and vice versa, since the two terms are necessarily relational and interdependent (Fuss, 1991; Sedgwick, 1990; see also Weedon, 1987, p. 23 on Saussure's "sign theory"). In other words, straightness does not exist separately from gayness but is in fact defined by it (and vice versa). Furthermore, sexual identity is experienced or accomplished "in a particular class-, race-, or gender-mediated way, and only so" (Seidman, 1993, pp. 136-137); likewise, cultural identity is "done" differently depending on one's sexual identity (see Mac An Ghaill, 1994). When identities are understood to be not just multiple but mutually inflecting (see Pallotta-Chiarolli, 1996; Phelan, 1994), it becomes clear that to understand the workings of any domain of identity (e.g., gender) it is necessary to consider that domain as part of, or in relation to, the domain of sexual identity. Lastly, according to queer theorists the significance of the hetero/homosexual binary extends far beyond identities. This binary is a pervasive, shaping force throughout "Western" knowledges and discourses. Its cultural significance is as great as other powerful binaries such as masculine/feminine or bourgeois/proletariat (Sedgwick, 1990). Thus, classifying sexual identities involves more than just sexualities but extends to cultural patterns of thinking and living.

The application of queer theory to teaching or training contexts allows for acknowledgment that issues pertaining to sexual identities might be relevant to anyone, not just gay people, and for a range of reasons. This wider focus allows everyone, whatever their own positioning with regard to sexual identity, to participate in and contribute to the discussion. This may also help to counter any tendency to reductively construct people as either toler*ated* or toler*ant* (see Britzman, 1995, pp. 159-160). Also, considering sexual identity and other "acts of identity" as interconnected, even mutually constitutive, underscores the broad relevance of matters pertaining to sexual identities. Furthermore, learning opportunities are opened up when the hetero/homosexual binary is seen as working on and in a wide range of social and cultural practices, not just sexualities.

Looking at How Certain Sexual Identities Are (or Are Not) Made to Seem Normal

Of primary concern within lesbian/gay identity-based theory and politics has been the promotion of tolerance and social justice in order to challenge and transform prejudicial attitudes (homophobia) and discriminatory systems and actions (heterosexism). Queer theorists, however, are concerned with analyzing cultural knowledges and discourses: "The roots of heterosexism are not socialization, prejudice, tradition, or scapegoating, but a basic way of organizing knowledges and fields of daily life which are deeply articulated in the core social practices of Western societies" (Seidman, 1995, p. 135). Queer theorists have therefore coined the term "heteronormativity," which refers to making heterosexuality–and only heterosexuality–seem normal or natural (Warner, 1993).

Identifying norms and analyzing how they operate may prove useful educationally for several reasons. First of all, the focus is not on whether a particular sexual identity is normal or natural, or even whether it *should* be considered natural, but on what makes it *seem* natural (or unnatural). (This follows Foucault's [1980, p. 118] interest not in discovering "truth" but in analyzing how "the effects of truth" are produced.) The point is not so much to debate as to analyze. Secondly, attempting to identify cultural and linguistic norms makes it possible to recognize not only prevailing norms but also competing norms. In linguistically and/or culturally heterogeneous groups it may be especially important to underscore the fact that norms are not static or universal but context-specific, changing, and contested. Lastly, and perhaps most importantly, making norms explicit enables people to make choices that are more informed and therefore more strategic as they position themselves in relation to those norms.

A FOCUS ON INQUIRY

An emphasis on inclusion, which adds subordinate sexual identities and aims to validate them, may be less effective than an emphasis on inquiry, which seeks to understand how language, culture, and social interactions operate with respect to all sexual identities. An inquiry approach follows queer theory in theorizing sexual identities as acts rather than facts, problematizing all sexual identities rather than legitimizing subordinate ones, recognizing the broad significance of sexual identities, and looking at how certain sexual identities are (or are not) made to seem normal. In culturally and linguistically diverse groups, a focus on investigating sexual identities as socially situated practices may be more useful than a focus on promoting "tolerance" of those who identify as gay. Educationally, the aim, as Burbules (1997, p. 111) puts it, should not be "[t]olerance of difference, or for that matter celebrations of difference," but "the critical re-examination of difference, the questioning of our own systems of difference, and what they mean for ourselves and for other people." It is this sort of inquiry that a queer theory approach invites.

REFERENCES

Anderson, A. et al. [a total of 26 signatories] (1997, August/September). [Letter to the editor]. *TESOL Matters, 7* (4), 22.

Austin, J. L. (1962). *How to do things with words.* London: Oxford University Press.

Brems, M., & Strauss, E. (1995). *Homophobia in the classroom: Examining a teacher's role.* Workshop presented at the 29th Annual Teachers of English to Speakers of Other Languages Convention, Long Beach, CA.

Britzman, D. (1995). Is there a queer pedagogy? Or, stop reading straight. *Educational Theory, 45*(2), 151-165.

Burbules, N.C. (1997). A grammar of difference: Some ways of rethinking difference and diversity as educational topics. *Australian Educational Researcher, 24*(1), 97-116.

Butler, J. (1990). *Gender trouble: Feminism and the subversion of identity.* New York: Routledge.

Butler, J. (1991). Imitation and gender insubordination. In D. Fuss (Ed.), *Inside/Out: Lesbian theories, gay theories* (pp. 13-31). London: Routledge.

Carscadden, L., Nelson, C., & Ward, J. (1992). *We are your colleagues: Lesbian and gay issues in ESL.* Colloquium presented at the 26th Annual Teachers of English to Speakers of Other Languages Convention, Vancouver, Canada.

Censotti, E. (1998). Out in the classroom. *Outside In . . . The Newsletter of the Lesbian/Gay/Bisexual and Friends Caucus of TESOL, 4*(1), 11.

Cummings, M.C., & Nelson, C. (1993). Our time has come: TESOL forms lesbian/gay/bisexual task force, Part I. *TESOL Matters, 3*(4), 5.

Destandau, N., Nelson, C., & Snelbecker, K. (1995). *Coming out in the classroom: Equal educational opportunities.* Colloquium presented at the 29th Annual teachers of English to Speakers of Other Languages Convention, Long Beach, CA.

Epstein, D. (Ed.). (1994). *Challenging lesbian and gay inequalities in education.* Buckingham: Open University Press.

Foucault, M. (1980). *Power/Knowledge: Selected interviews and other writings, 1927-1977.* (C. Gordon, L. Marshall, J. Mepham, & K. Soper, Trans.). New York: Pantheon.

Foucault, M. (1990). *The history of sexuality, volume 1*. New York: Random House.

Fuss, D. (1991). Inside/Out. In D. Fuss (Ed.), *Inside/Out: Lesbian theories, gay theories* (pp. 1-10). New York: Routledge.

Garber, L. (Ed.). (1994). *Tilting the tower: Lesbians/Teaching/Queer subjects*. New York: Routledge.

Gumperz, J.J., & Cook-Gumperz, J. (1982). Introduction: Language and the communication of social identity. In J.J. Gumperz (Ed.), *Language and social identity* (pp. 1-21). Cambridge: Cambridge University Press.

Hanson, J. (1998). A unit on romance, marriage, and sexual orientation. *Outside In . . . The Newsletter of the Lesbian/Gay/Bisexual and Friends Caucus of TESOL, 3*(2), 5-6.

Harris, S. (1990). *Lesbian and gay issues in the English classroom: The importance of being honest*. Philadelphia: Open University Press.

Hart, E. (1989). *Literacy and the empowerment of lesbian and gay students*. Paper presented at the Conference on College Composition and Communication, Seattle (ERIC Reproduction No. ED 304 662).

Hirst, A. (1981). Gay's the word but not in EFL. *EFL Gazette, 28* (reprinted in TESOL Newsletter, 1982, June).

Jones, C., & Jack, D. (1994). *Inclusion: Gay and lesbian issues and literature in ESL classes*. Workshop presented at the 28th Annual TESOL Convention, Baltimore, MD.

Kappra, R. (1998/1999). Addressing heterosexism in the IEP [Intensive English Program] classroom. *TESOL Matters, 8*(6), 19.

Kato, N. (1999, Fall/Winter). Working with gay, lesbian and bisexual international students in the United States. *International Educator [NAFSA: Association of International Educators] 8*(1) [Available: http://www.nafsa.org].

Laskey, L., & Beavis, C. (Eds.). (1996). *Schooling and sexualities: Teaching for a positive sexuality*. Deakin Centre for Education and Change, Deakin University.

Le Page, R.B., & Tabouret-Keller, A. (1985). *Acts of identity*. Cambridge: Cambridge University Press.

Livia, A., & Hall, K. (1997). "It's a girl!": Bringing performativity back to linguistics. In A. Livia & K. Hall (Eds.), *Queerly phrased: Language, gender, and sexuality* (pp. 3-18). New York: Oxford University Press.

Mac An Ghaill, M. (1994). (In)visibility: Sexuality, race and masculinity in the school context. In D. Epstein (Ed.), *Challenging lesbian and gay inequalities in education* (pp. 152-176). Buckingham: Open University Press.

Malinowitz, H. (1995). *Textual orientations: Lesbian and gay students and the making of discourse communities*. Portsmouth, NH: Heinemann.

Mittler, M.L., & Blumenthal, A. (1994). On being a change agent: Teacher as text, homophobia as context. In L. Garber (Ed.), *Tilting the tower: Lesbian/Teaching/Queer subjects* (pp. 3-10). New York: Routledge.

Neff, J. (1992). *Confronting heterosexism in the classroom*. Workshop presented at the International Association of Teachers of English as a Foreign Language, Lille, France.

Nelson, C. (1993a). Heterosexism in ESL: Examining our attitudes. *TESOL Quarterly, 27*(1), 143-150.

Nelson, C. (1993b). Our time has come: TESOL forms lesbian/gay/bisexual task force, Part II. *TESOL Matters*, *3*(5), 23.

Nelson, C. (1999). Sexual identities in ESL: Queer theory and classroom inquiry. *TESOL Quarterly*, *33*(3), 371-391.

Nelson, C. (2000). *Sexual identities and language pedagogy: Lesbian/Gay content in ESL*. Unpublished doctoral thesis. Macquarie University, Sydney.

Pallotta-Chiarolli, M. (1996). "A rainbow in my heart": Interweaving ethnicity and sexuality studies. In Laskey, L. & C. Beavis (Eds.), *Schooling and sexualities: Teaching for a positive sexuality* (pp. 53-67). Deakin Centre for Education and Change, Deakin University.

Parmeter, S.H., & Reti, I. (Eds.). (1988). *The lesbian in front of the classroom*. Santa Cruz: HerBooks.

Phelan, S. (1994). *Getting specific: Postmodern lesbian politics*. Minneapolis: University of Minnesota Press.

Phillips, D. (1996). Agency and identity in the gay and lesbian studies classroom: A perspective from Australia. In Walling, D.R. (Ed.), *Open lives, safe schools: Addressing gay and lesbian issues in education* (pp. 103-120). Bloomington, IN: Phi Delta Kappa Educational Foundation.

Poynton, C. (1997). Language, difference and identity: Three perspectives. *Literacy and Numeracy Studies*, *7*(1), 7-24.

Saint Pierre, R. (1994). On being out in the classroom: Dilemma or duty? In Jennings, K. (Ed.), *One teacher in 10: Gay and lesbian educators tell their stories* (pp. 164-167). Boston: Alyson Publications.

Sears, J.T. (Ed.). (1992). *Sexuality and the curriculum*. New York: Teachers College Press.

Sedgwick, E.K. (1990). *Epistemology of the closet*. London: Penguin.

Seidman, S. (1993). Identity and politics in a "postmodern" gay culture: Some historical and conceptual notes. In M. Warner (Ed.), *Fear of a queer planet: Queer politics and social theory* (pp. 105-142). Minneapolis: University of Minnesota Press.

Seidman, S. (1995). Deconstructing queer theory or the under-theorization of the social and the ethical. In L. Nicholson & S. Seidman (Eds.), *Social postmodernism: Beyond identity politics* (pp. 116-141). Cambridge: Cambridge University Press.

Shore, E. (1992 June). "Out of the closet and into the classroom": A personal essay on coming out to my students. *GLESOL Newsletter [The Newsletter of Gay and Lesbian Educators to Speakers of Other Languages]*, *1*(1), 3-4.

Snelbecker, K.A. (1994). *Speaking out: A survey of gay, lesbian and bisexual teachers of ESOL*. Master's thesis, School for International Training, Brattleboro, VT. ERIC Clearinghouse on Language and Linguistics Database #ED375680.

Sumara, D., & Davis, B. (1999). Interrupting heteronormativity: Toward a queer curriculum theory. *Curriculum Inquiry*, *29*(2), 191.

Summerhawk, B. (1998). From closet to classroom: Gay issues in ESL/EFL. *The Language Teacher (JALT)*, *22*(5), 21-23.

Warner, M. (1993). Introduction. In Warner, M. (Ed.), *Fear of a queer planet: Queer politics and social theory* (pp. vii-xxxi). Minneapolis: University of Minnesota Press.

Weedon, C. (1987). *Feminist practice and poststructuralist theory*. London: Blackwell.

A Reflection of Resistance. Discourses of Heterosexism and Homophobia in Teacher Training Classrooms

Kerry H. Robinson
Tania Ferfolja

SUMMARY. Training pre-service teachers about lesbian and gay issues and heterosexism is crucial to counteracting the harassment of young people and teachers in schools, in promoting social change and enhancing the quality of life of lesbian and gay individuals. However, this discussion focuses on pre-service teachers' resistance to addressing lesbian and gay issues in schooling. The forms of resistance encountered are many, and include the personal perception of the relevance of lesbian and gay issues to teaching in schools and the various discourses in which these perceptions are situated. This discussion reflects upon the experiences of the authors, who have taught social justice issues in education to pre-service teachers in a metropolitan university in Sydney, Australia. *[Article copies available for a fee from The Haworth Document Delivery Service: 1-800-HAWORTH. E-mail address: <getinfo@haworthpressinc.com> Website: <http://www.HaworthPress.com> © 2002 by The Haworth Press, Inc. All rights reserved.]*

Kerry H. Robinson, PhD, MA, BA, DipEd, is affiliated with the School of Education and Early Childhood Studies, University of Western Sydney, Bankstown Campus, Building 4, Locked Bag 1797, Penrith DC, NSW 1797, Australia (E-mail: k.robinson@uws.edu.au). Tania Ferfolja, MA, BEd, is affiliated with The Learning Centre, University of New South Wales, Sydney 2052, Australia (E-mail: t.ferfolja@unsw.edu.au).

[Haworth co-indexing entry note]: "A Reflection of Resistance. Discourses of Heterosexism and Homophobia in Teacher Training Classrooms." Robinson, Kerry H., and Tania Ferfolja. Co-published simultaneously in *Journal of Gay & Lesbian Social Services* (Harrington Park Press, an imprint of The Haworth Press, Inc.) Vol. 14, No. 2, 2002, pp. 55-64; and: *From Here to Diversity: The Social Impact of Lesbian and Gay Issues in Education in Australia and New Zealand* (ed: Kerry H. Robinson, Jude Irwin, and Tania Ferfolja) Harrington Park Press, an imprint of The Haworth Press, Inc., 2002, pp. 55-64. Single or multiple copies of this article are available for a fee from The Haworth Document Delivery Service [1-800-HAWORTH, 9:00 a.m. - 5:00 p.m. (EST). E-mail address: getinfo@haworthpressinc.com].

KEYWORDS. Teacher training, pre-service teachers, resistance, lesbian, gay, heterosexism, homophobia, normalization, sexuality, discourse

INTRODUCTION

Homophobia and heterosexism are major social justice issues, which often result in discrimination, inequality, and violence. These phenomena are prevalent and operate to police the rigid boundaries around gender and sexuality, limiting the ways in which they are represented and experienced. Hence, these limitations have implications not just for those who identify or are identified as lesbian or gay, but also for the way that all individuals live and express their sexual identities. As a consequence, dealing with lesbian and gay issues is essential in pre-service teacher training and more broadly within social and community services. Even though anti-homophobia education is relevant and important to the well-being of all individuals, this paper highlights the fact that many pre-service teachers actually resist the notion of dealing with such issues in schools. The discussion is based on the authors' experiences of teaching social justice issues in education, to early childhood, primary and high school pre-service teachers at an Australian metropolitan university. This paper focuses on the lesbian and gay component of that teaching unit.

Teacher trainees are not a homogeneous group, but come with their own varied perceptions and prejudices around issues of difference. Dealing with gay and lesbian issues in schools is a contentious issue reflecting the dominant socio-cultural, moral, and religious discourses that prevail around sexuality in society. Thus, enhancing pre-service teachers' understandings of the complexities of these issues is a challenging task as they are positioned within the various complex and often contradictory range of discourses pertaining to sexuality and sexual minorities. We identify some of the ways in which many pre-service teachers resist dealing with lesbian and gay issues. These resistances include: the drawing on various popular mythologies and misconceptions that abound in relation to lesbians and gay men that promote discrimination; the personal perceptions of the relevance of lesbian and gay issues to teaching in schools; individual understandings of what constitutes a "good" teacher and their positioning within these discourses; the utilization of discourses around religious, moral, family, and cultural values; the perception of, and rejection of, "pandering to vocal minorities";

the notion that social justice, in particular lesbian and gay issues, receives too much attention; the pathologization and normalization of harassment and discrimination; and the fear of one's sexuality being "read" as lesbian or gay by association.

POSITIONING THE DISCUSSION: WHY DEAL WITH SEXUALITIES IN PRE-SERVICE EDUCATION?

Dominant discourses of sexuality and gender in schools and society more broadly perpetuate heterosexuality as the "norm" whilst constructing those who are nonheterosexual as deviant and abnormal. In schools, teachers and students are often targets for homophobic harassment and violence because they do not comply with hegemonic constructions of masculinity and femininity (Robinson, 1996). Epstein and Johnson (1998) point out that heterosexuality is constructed around dominant discourses of gender. This understanding of gender is highlighted in Butler's theory (1990) that suggests that gender needs to be read within the context of a "heterosexual matrix" in which gender is defined and limited within terms of compulsory heterosexuality. The construction of the heterosexual/homosexual binarism (Sedgwick, 1990) defines homosexuals as "other," perpetuating the discrimination, prejudice, and violence experienced by individuals who identify as, or are positioned by others as, lesbian or gay. Consequently, the deconstruction of this hierarchical binary relationship, heterosexual us/homosexual them, and of the discourses in which it is constituted, is crucial to establishing a more equitable society and needs to be included in a social justice education framework.

Failing to disrupt such social binaries can have far-reaching effects on the individual who is "othered" in these relationships. Discrimination can impact negatively on the daily lives of individuals, particularly youth, in terms of their educational achievements, their social development, their family relationships and their health (Irwin, Gregoric & Winter, 1997). Homophobic prejudice and discrimination has also been identified as a factor in the high incidence of youth suicide and suicide ideation amongst lesbian and gay youth in western countries (Denborough, 1996; Mac An Ghaill, 1994). It has also been the cause of violent hate crimes, epitomized by the recent murder of Matthew Shepard in Laramie, Wyoming, in the United States. In the U.S. gay-related hate crimes have increased, with the violence being predominantly instigated by young teenage men (Chasnoff & Cohen, 1997). As pointed out, this behaviour is intimately linked with dominant constructions of and representations of hegemonic masculinity (Connell, 1995) within the "heterosexual matrix" (Butler, 1990).

However, it is not only students who experience homophobia. Lesbian- and gay-identified teachers, as well as those who are perceived to be nonheterosexual, experience violence and vilification in their position as teachers, not only in their work environment but also in their homes (Ferfolja, 1998; Robinson, 1996). Thus, the need to address homophobia in schooling as part of a social justice framework, beginning in early childhood educational settings, is crucial.

Although many people consider that children are "too young" to understand or participate in prejudice and discrimination, research has indicated that very young children also espouse homophobic and heterosexist sentiments (Bickmore, 1999; Chasnoff & Cohen, 1997; Walkerdine, 1990). Teachers need a critical understanding of the socio-cultural and political power relationships within the constructions of gender and sexuality which can inform their strategies to positively deal with gay and lesbian issues in their pedagogical practice (Robinson & Jones Diaz, 1999). In order to achieve this, it is imperative that university teacher training programs include a critical understanding of gay and lesbian issues and the discourses that perpetuate inequality and discrimination.

However, teacher educators encounter various forms of resistance amongst many of the pre-service teachers whom they teach. Pre-service teachers' responses to lesbian and gay issues and their potential implementation in schooling are complex and contradictory, shifting and unstable. They are impacted by a number of factors outlined below, which, although they are discussed separately, often intersect with each other.

RESISTANCES TO DEALING WITH LESBIAN AND GAY ISSUES

Mythologies and Misconceptions

There are many myths around lesbian and gay identities that are espoused by pre-service teachers in teacher training classrooms and which reflect broader socio-cultural misconceptions. These include the notion that lesbians and gay men are hypersexual and will make sexual advances towards anyone of the same sex. This perspective completely disregards the fact that many lesbians and gay men are silent or totally closeted about their sexuality (Hinson, 1996). In addition, these misunderstandings fuel misconceptions of lesbians and gays as recruiters to their sexuality. This perception is intensified when dealing with youth who are positioned in discourses of childhood innocence and who are considered vulnerable. The "recruitment" fallacy is further exacerbated by the popular myth that "homosexuals" are inherently pedophilic. Yet, ironically, "survivors" of child sexual abuse are generally female and their perpetrators are most often heterosexual males (Easteal, 1994), which dispels the myth that links "homosexuals" as the main sexual predators of children.

Discourses of the "Good Teacher" and the Importance of Being "Value Neutral"

The discourse of the "good teacher," which focuses on the mechanics of teaching, and in particular, classroom control, is perceived as paramount to pre-service teacher training and often eclipses the perceived importance and relevance of dealing with equity issues of any kind (Robinson & Ferfolja, 2001). This discourse is frequently reinforced by the belief that what constitutes "good teaching" is value-free pedagogy and that teachers cannot be seen to "support" controversial social justice issues in particular.

However, schools and teachers are not value-neutral and, through their philosophies, pedagogies, and the overt and covert curricula, often perpetuate and constitute the prevailing dominant socio-cultural discourses operating within society that reinforce inequalities. The discrimination, silences, and marginalization around lesbian and gay issues in schooling are just one example of the way this process operates. In addition, teachers are subjectively positioned within these discourses and hence bring their own beliefs and prejudices to the classroom. Consequently, it is imperative that pre-service teachers recognize that as individuals, their practices are often value-laden. In fact, the "good" teacher is one who is aware of their potential to reinforce and perpetuate inequality and discrimination through exclusive practices or a failure to identify and sensitively deal with social justice issues. Furthermore, a "good" teacher is not only aware, but also pro-active in their role to ensure equity. Thus, pre-service teachers need to be educated about the politics of difference and how it operates in schools and the broader society, and to be able to deconstruct discourses that constitute inequalities.

Issues of Religion, Morality, and Cultural Values

One's religious, moral, and cultural values often influence the pre-service teachers' perspectives in dealing with lesbian and gay issues. The social order in most cultures is based around explicit and implicit taboos, rules and regulations in regards to sexuality that stem from dominant discourses that uphold dominant values, and link (hetero)sexuality to marriage, procreation, and family. This social order is often reinforced by religious doctrine and practices (Herdt, 1997).

However, pre-service teachers' relationships with dominant religious, cultural, and moral values around lesbian and gay issues are multiple and complex, and resistances based on these perspectives vary. For example, some pre-service teachers who are positioned within religious and moral discourses that oppose nonheterosexual relationships find a way to reconcile their beliefs with their role as teacher as "good Samaritan," and take up more egalitarian discourses from which to read gay and lesbian issues. In contrast, others are positioned in particularly strong anti-lesbian/gay moral, cultural, and religious discourses, and their resistance is extreme and frequently vocal and aggressive. Often, their resistances are linked to the myths and stereotypes discussed earlier.

Further, many pre-service teachers maintain that sexuality issues, particularly those that challenge the heterosexual status quo, should be dealt with in the privacy of the family, which is perceived to be the main teacher of children's moral education. There is a strong notion that as a potential teacher, one should not broach lesbian and gay issues, because they may conflict with parental morals. Ironically, contradictions are demonstrated amongst pre-service teachers when inequality and discrimination are placed within contexts other than sexuality. Some are more willing to assume a social justice position in their future teaching practice, even if it means challenging the beliefs and moral values of parents, when it comes to other issues such as racism and/or sexism. For some, lesbian and gay concerns transcend the definition of what constitutes an "appropriate" social justice issue.

Special Interest Groups and "Vocal Minorities"

Labeling lesbian and gay issues as the domain of "vocal minorities" and "special interest groups" is a way of marginalizing and repositioning this social justice issue as "other" and in effect not relevant or important to the daily lives of the visible majority. This resistance is frequently constituted within the "majority heterosexual us/minority homosexual them" binarism. Some dispute the need to understand "the politics of vocal minorities". As one pre-service teacher commented, "I sometimes think that the will of the majority is lost in the louder voices of special interest groups." In addition, positive discrimination in the form of anti-vilification and anti-discrimination legislation, which is aimed at addressing inequality towards lesbians and gays, is often considered by some as problematic and discriminatory in itself. It is perceived that this form of legislation favors a minority group over the needs of the majority; that is, somebody who is challenging the "acceptable" and going beyond the norm is provided state protection for doing so. Foucault (1977) highlights that society rewards those who conform to the "norm" and punishes those who deviate from the socially constructed boundaries of acceptable behaviour. However, in the case of positive discrimination around homosexuality, the person who deviates from the "norm" is seen to be rewarded with protective legislation.

In addition, minority sexuality issues are often considered to have no relevance to the lives of the majority of students in the future classrooms of pre-service teachers or to constructions of heterosexuality more generally (Britzman, 1997). There seems to be an almost unquestionable assumption that all students are heterosexual. Thus, pre-service teachers often consider that learning about lesbian and gay issues is irrelevant to their future teaching to the perceived heterosexual, "majority" culture (Robinson & Ferfolja, 2001). However, understanding gay and lesbian discrimination is not only of benefit to a perceived "minority" of students. Deconstruction of the sexual binary, "heterosexual us/homosexual them," allows one to understand the confinement and limitations of all sexual and gender relationships, including heterosexuality, and the ways they are policed and reinforced (Sedgwick, 1990).

Some students' resistance reflects their belief that issues pertaining to social justice are "done to death"; that is, there is a notion such issues are "forced upon" individuals by "politically correct" others. Lesbian and gay issues, in particular, are perceived by some as getting more than their fair share of the curriculum "space" and succumbing to the needs of special interest groups. Those who deal with lesbian and gay issues are read as being on their "soapbox" or "pushing their own agenda." Unlike other areas of social justice, lesbian and gay issues are perceived as being "overdone" or allocated too much time.

Sexuality by Association

Recently, a young male pre-service teacher expressed concern that dealing with lesbian and gay issues would potentially label him as gay, even though he was genuinely keen to promote a critical social justice pedagogy in his future classroom. His concern was based on the fact that his association with a gay acquaintance was questioned by significant and long-term friends in his sporting/social life, resulting in a degree of harassment and his subsequent shifting away from any interaction with the gay man. Dominant constructions of masculinity serve not only to "other" the gay man, but also to question the masculinity and sexuality of the pre-service teacher, because of his association (Kimmel, 1994).

This fear of being positioned as lesbian or gay by association is not uncommon, especially amongst young men, where their masculinity and sexuality are constructed within the rigid boundaries of hegemonic masculinity. Despite an awareness that a social justice perspective is important to their professional standing and that sexuality-based discrimination is common, their resistance comes from the fear of being potentially labeled as "gay," and harassed and marginalized not only by their friends, but moreover, by future students and colleagues. There is an awareness of the surveillance and stigma experienced by those perceived to be lesbian or gay in society, and many pre-service teachers are particularly conscious of the fact that they do not want to experience similar discrimination because of their associations.

Blaming the Victim

Much student resistance centers around the discourse that blames the "victim" for any harassment and/or violence experienced (Robinson & Ferfolja, 2001). For example, some pre-service teachers approach lesbian/gay sexualities from pathologizing and marginalizing perspectives that condone abuse. Lesbians and gay males are often perceived as inherently "abnormal" or "sick." In this process, lesbians/gays become demonized because of their sexuality and seen as ultimately responsible for the harassment inflicted upon them. Similarly, sexuality when perceived to be an individual choice, or socially constructed, results in lesbians and gays being marginalized and derided as deviant or perverted, because they have chosen an alternative sexuality and therefore deserve the "punishment" they receive (Foucault, 1977). Some pre-service teachers claim that, in this context, if so desired, lesbians and gay males could ultimately choose to conform to the normalized majority heterosexual culture, thus avoiding violence and vilification.

"Victim" blaming is also particularly prevalent when those harassed do not fit dominant heterosexual stereotypes (Robinson & Ferfolja 2001). Individuals who portray more overt lesbian/gay stereotyped characteristics challenge the boundaries of hegemonic gender constructions. Thus, for many pre-service teachers, being gay/lesbian is considered more "tolerable," if individuals do not transgress popularly maintained gender "norms." It is perceived by some that "difference" should not be "flaunted" and those who flout their "different" sexuality "deserve what they get." There is a strong heterosexist discourse that if harassed individuals "changed themselves" to look, sound, and act like their heterosexual peers they would be accepted more readily.

In addition, "normalization" of harassment is another way that some pre-service teachers justify schoolyard harassment against those who identify or are perceived to be lesbian or gay. There is a common belief that "all students are harassed," that it is a part of "growing up" and that they need to "learn to survive." Consequently, all forms of harassment or discrimination are perceived to be similar and are frequently viewed apolitically and labelled as childhood "bullying."

CONCLUSION

As a teacher educator one is frequently defending the inclusion of sexuality issues as relevant and essential for teacher education. This far exceeds the justification required for other topics. Regardless, teacher educators are in a unique position to challenge discourses that foster discrimination, hatred, and fear around sexual difference, by encouraging pre-service teachers to critically reflect and examine their own subjective positions within discourses of sexuality. This discussion has outlined many of the key resistances that some pre-service teachers express when dealing with lesbian and gay issues. Acknowledging, understanding, and dealing with such resistances and contradictions is crucial in addressing the serious and widespread problem of anti-lesbian/gay violence and vilification in schools and the broader community.

REFERENCES

Bickmore, K. (1999). Why discuss sexuality in elementary school? In W.J. Letts IV & J.T. Sears (Eds.), *Queering elementary education: Advancing the dialogue about sexualities and schooling* (pp. 15-26). Lanham: Rowman & Littlefield Publishers Inc.

Britzman, D. P. (1997). What is this thing called love? New discourses for understanding gay and lesbian youth. In S. de Castell, & M. Bryson (Eds.), *Radical* *in<ter>ventions: Identity, politics, and difference/s in educational praxis* (pp. 183-210). Albany: State University of New York Press.

Butler, J. (1990). *Gender trouble: Feminism and the subversion of identity.* New York: Routledge.

Chasnoff, D., & Cohen, H. (Producers). (1997). *It's elementary: Talking about gay issues in school* [video]. (Available from Women's Educational Media, USA).

Connell, R.W. (1995). *Masculinities.* Sydney: Allen & Unwin.

Denborough, D. (1996). Power and partnership? Challenging the sexual construction of schooling. In L. Laskey & C. Beavis (Eds.), *Schooling and Sexualities* (pp. 1-10). Victoria: Deakin Centre for Education and Change, Deakin University.

Easteal, P. (1994). *Voices of the survivors.* Australia: Spinifex Press.

Epstein, D., & Johnson, R. (1998). *Schooling sexualities.* Buckingham: Open University Press.

Ferfolja, T. (1998). Australian lesbian teachers–a reflection of homophobic harassment of high school teachers in New South Wales government schools. *Gender and Education 10* (4), 401-415.

Foucault, M. (1977). *Discipline and punish: The birth of the prison.* London: Allen Lane.

Herdt, G. (1997). *Same sex, different cultures: Gays and lesbians across cultures.* Boulder: Westview Press.

Hinson, S. (1996). A practice focussed approach to addressing heterosexist violence in Australian schools. In L. Laskey & C. Beavis (Eds.), *Schooling and Sexualities* (pp. 1-10). Victoria: Deakin Centre for Education and Change, Deakin University.

Irwin, J., Gregoric, M., & Winter, B. (1997). Violence against homeless young lesbians. In G. Mason & S. Tomsen (Eds.), *Homophobic violence.* Sydney: The Hawkins Press.

Kimmel, M.S. (1994). Masculinity as homophobia: Fear, shame, and silence in the construction of gender identity. In H. Brod & M. Kaufman (Eds.), *Theorizing masculinities* (pp. 119-141). Thousand Oaks: Sage Publications.

Mac An Ghaill, M. (1994). *The making of men: Masculinities, sexualities and schooling.* Buckingham: Open University Press.

Robinson, K.H. (1996). *Sexual harassment in secondary schools.* Unpublished doctoral dissertation, University of New South Wales, Australia.

Robinson, K.H., & Jones Diaz, C. (1999). Doing theory with early childhood educators: Understanding difference and diversity in personal and professional contexts. *Australian Journal of Early Childhood, 24*(4), 33-40.

Robinson, K.H., & Ferfolja, T. (2001). "What are we doing this for?" Dealing with lesbian and gay issues in teacher education. *British Journal of Sociology of Education, 22*(1), 121-134.

Sedgwick, E. (1990). *Epistemology of the closet.* Berkeley: University of California Press.

Walkerdine, V. (1990). *Sex, power and pedagogy.* London: Verso.

Discrimination Against Gay Men, Lesbians, and Transgender People Working in Education

Jude Irwin

SUMMARY. This paper explores the workplace experiences of 120 gay men, lesbians, and transgender people who were employed as teachers, academics, and educators. The data, drawn from a larger collaborative research project, explored the workplace experiences of 900 gay men, lesbians, and transgender people. Homophobic harassment and treatment were widespread amongst the lesbian, gay men, and transgender teachers, academics, and educators. The paper will utilize the stories of those who experienced discrimination to explicate the issues confronting gay men, lesbians, and transgender people who work in the education system. *[Article copies available for a fee from The Haworth Document Delivery Service: 1-800-HAWORTH. E-mail address: <getinfo@haworthpressinc.com> Website: <http://www.HaworthPress.com> © 2002 by The Haworth Press, Inc. All rights reserved.]*

KEYWORDS. Lesbian, gay, transgender, discrimination, education, homophobia, academic, schools, employment, teachers

---

Jude Irwin is Associate Professor in the Department of Social Work, Social Policy and Sociology, University of Sydney, NSW 2006, Australia (E-mail: jude.irwin@social.usyd.edu.au).

[Haworth co-indexing entry note]: "Discrimination Against Gay Men, Lesbians, and Transgender People Working in Education." Irwin, Jude. Co-published simultaneously in *Journal of Gay & Lesbian Social Services* (Harrington Park Press, an imprint of The Haworth Press, Inc.) Vol. 14, No. 2, 2002, pp. 65-77; and: *From Here to Diversity: The Social Impact of Lesbian and Gay Issues in Education in Australia and New Zealand* (ed: Kerry H. Robinson, Jude Irwin, and Tania Ferfolja) Harrington Park Press, an imprint of The Haworth Press, Inc., 2002, pp. 65-77. Single or multiple copies of this article are available for a fee from The Haworth Document Delivery Service [1-800-HAWORTH, 9:00 a.m. - 5:00 p.m. (EST). E-mail address: getinfo@haworthpressinc.com].

Homophobic discrimination in the workplace has been on the political agenda of lesbians and gay men in Australia since the early 1970s, when a group of gay and lesbian activists voiced concerns about the discriminatory employment practices in the armed forces and when some gay men and lesbians were dismissed from their employment after they "came out" publicly (Irwin, 1999). More recently, research undertaken in Australia has confirmed the existence of homophobic discrimination in the workplace (e.g., Anti Discrimination Board, 1982, 1990, 1992; Gays and Lesbians Against Discrimination, 1994; New South Wales Gay and Lesbian Rights Lobby, 1992, 1994). Anecdotal evidence suggests that many gay, lesbian, and transgender teachers, academics, and educators have experienced extensive homophobic harassment and discrimination in the workplace, but there has been little documented research focusing specifically on their workplace experiences. This article is an attempt to address this gap. It explores the workplace experiences of 120 gay men, lesbians, and transgender teachers, academics, or educators who participated in a larger research project undertaken in 1997, which inquired into the workplace experiences of gay men, lesbians, and transgender people in Australia. The article will begin by outlining the methodology of the larger project and briefly reporting on the major findings. It will then highlight the experiences of teachers, academics, and educators, utilizing their narratives to provide more detailed understandings of the nature and effects of this discrimination.

THE LARGER RESEARCH PROJECT– AN OVERVIEW OF THE METHODOLOGY

The larger research project undertaken in 1997 explored the workplace experiences (current and previous) of gay men, lesbians, and transgender people (Irwin, 1999). The research was undertaken in Australia with almost all the participants coming from the populous east coast states of New South Wales and Victoria. The main aim of the research was to identify both the extent of discrimination in the workplace against gay men, lesbians, and transgender people and to increase understanding of this by exploring gay men's, lesbian's, and transgender people's experiences of discrimination in terms of collegial relationships, effects on career, and the impact these experiences had on health and overall well-being. It also explored the responses of unions and employers and assessed the adequacy of legal and other responses to discrimination. The research utilized a combination of both quantitative and qualitative methods. These included a self-completion survey (900 completed) from which the quantitative data were obtained, five focus group interviews, and 52 individual interviews.

The survey was advertised extensively in the gay, lesbian, and transgender media as well as in various community newsletters and in some mainstream specialist publications. It was distributed through venues, bookshops, cafes, gyms, and community organizations and services. A full copy of the survey was printed in a publication disseminated widely to members of the gay, lesbian, and transgender communities, and this resulted in over 300 responses. The survey explored the experiences of gay men, lesbians, and transgender people in their current or most recent workplace in great detail, including experiences of homophobic harassment and discrimination. Experiences of harassment and discrimination were also explored in previous workplaces. The survey included questions on the social and demographic backgrounds of participants; their educational and work experiences; experiences of discrimination (if relevant) and details of the discrimination, for example, who perpetrated it, what was done (if anything), to address the discrimination by either the participant, the employer, trade union, or other relevant organization); as well as the effects of the discrimination on the health, well-being, and employment options of the participant. The survey allowed for participants to elaborate on their responses with some opportunity for qualitative comments. It also gave participants the opportunity to participate in either an individual or a focus group interview. Focus group (5) and individual interviews (52) were undertaken in order to obtain a more in-depth understanding of the experiences of the participants. The focus group interviews aimed to capture the experiences of particular groups of gay men, lesbians, and transgender people. The five groups were conducted with lesbians who were living in a non-metropolitan area; gay men and lesbians who were "out" and had never experienced discrimination; gay men and lesbians who were out and who had experienced discrimination in a previous job; older gay men; and lesbians and transgender people who had taken action against workplace discrimination. Individual interviews were undertaken with twenty-seven lesbians, twenty gay men, and five transgender people. These explored in detail all aspects of the participant's workplace experiences. Those who had experienced workplace harassment or discrimination were given the opportunity to discuss what forms it took, its effects on their life generally, and the outcomes of any action they may have taken. If the participant had not experienced workplace discrimination, the focus of the interview was on identifying the positive aspects of the workplace.

The quantitative data from the survey were analyzed with the assistance of a software package and the use of descriptive statistics. The focus group and individual interviews were electronically recorded and summarized and, with the qualitative data obtained from the survey, analyzed thematically.

About the Participants

There were 900 participants in the research comprising 416 men, 415 women and 59 transgender people (20 were female to male, 39 were male to female). The majority of the participants (77%) were aged between 25 and 45. The participants were a highly educated group with over 67% (547) having completed a university degree. While lesbians overall had higher qualifications than gay men, they earned less, being over represented in the lowest salary groups and under represented in the highest salary groups. The participants were employed in a wide range of occupations with the most common being in administration (124 or 14%) and education (120 or 13%) and the least common in the unskilled (21 or 2%), security (17 or < 2%) and service areas (36 or 4%). The majority of the participants were Anglo Australian (74% or 664). One-third of the participants who did not identify as Anglo Australians came from non-English speaking countries (78 or < 9 %) with 3% (27) identifying as Indigenous Australians.

SUMMARY OF OVERALL FINDINGS

Participants identified both positive and negative workplace experiences. From the huge array of negative practices described there were two main categories. *Homophobic behavior, harassment, and discrimination* included homophobic jokes, verbal and physical harassment, destruction of property and threats which were directed at the participants. The perpetrators of this type of behavior were generally work colleagues or clients. *Prejudicial behavior, treatment, or practices* included such treatment as being overlooked for promotion, not being offered the same opportunities as heterosexual staff and the sabotaging of work. In some situations, the perpetrators were work colleagues at the same level as the victim but in many other situations they were employees in a supervisory position who had the power to decide who is offered opportunities (such as overtime, additional training, or good shifts). Another form of prejudicial treatment was a denial of entitlements available to heterosexual colleagues (such as partner superannuation, partner travel, and family health benefits).

The existence of discrimination in both current and previous workplaces of the participants was widespread, with 59% (532) of participants identifying experiences involving some form of homophobic behavior or prejudicial treatment in their current and/or previous workplaces. For almost all (97%) this was not just a single incident but was ongoing and affected the way they felt about themselves, their workplace, and their colleagues. It contributed to a hostile environment that had a powerful influence on their lives often extending beyond the workplace. Around 41% (368) of participants did not specify experiencing any discrimination in their current or previous workplaces and many of these identified positive workplace experiences.

The homophobic behavior reported by the participants included sexual and physical assault, verbal harassment and abuse, destruction of property, ridicule, belittling, and homophobic jokes. Prejudicial treatment in the workplace included unfair rosters, unreasonable work expectations, sabotaging and undermining of work, and restrictions to career. Forty-one participants considered they had been dismissed from their most recent job because of their homosexuality. Several participants also reported they had been denied workplace entitlements that were available to heterosexual colleagues such as partner travel, superannuation, and compassionate leave. Homophobic harassment and prejudicial treatment spanned all occupations, industries, and types and sizes of the employing organizations. However, discrimination was more likely to happen in traditionally male-dominated occupations and industries.

Transgender participants were most likely to experience discrimination or harassment (75% or 44). Just over 67% (248) of lesbians and 57% (236) of gay men experienced discrimination or harassment in their workplaces.

The effects of this homophobic behavior and prejudicial treatment were extensive and included effects on the individual and their workplace performance. The effects on individuals included increased stress, depression, illness, loss of self-confidence, increased alcohol and drug intake, and attempted suicide. Workplace performance was negatively affected as a result of increased leave due to stress-related illness, participants not wanting to be at work and having to be constantly on guard. The existence of homophobic behavior and harassment affected the workplace culture, often creating a hostile and unsafe environment for out or suspected lesbians, gay men, and transgender people.

Some participants commented that they did not experience homophobic discrimination because no one at their workplace knew they were gay or lesbian. While a high percentage of participants were out to at least someone in the workplace, 10% (90) chose not to tell anyone in their workplace that they were gay, lesbian, or transgender. Many participants were out selectively because they felt unsafe to be entirely open about their sexuality. Those participants who were out to everyone had often chosen workplaces where they felt safe and where "I can be myself." In these situations participants felt there was little likelihood of experiencing homophobic discrimination.

Only a small percentage of those people who were the recipients of homophobic harassment or behavior took action. Those who did take action were most likely to confront the harasser or discuss the issue with management. Very few participants chose to use the legal avenues that exist. The main contributing factors to this decision were the anticipated long time delays, exposure of their sexuality, and little chance of a positive outcome. Unions did not play a major role in assisting people to take action.

The positive workplace experiences of participants were characterized by a workplace culture which promoted difference (rather than just accepted or tolerated it), that is, where gays, lesbians and transgender people felt safe and where their contribution was acknowledged and valued.

WORKPLACE EXPERIENCES OF TEACHERS, ACADEMICS, AND EDUCATORS

Teachers, academics, and educators comprised the second-largest occupational group participating in the research (120 or 13%) after administrative workers (124 or 14%). They included those employed in the state and private (including church operated) school systems and those employed in the post secondary and tertiary education sectors. Just over 60% (71) of the teachers, academics, and educators identified experiencing homophobic behavior, harassment, and discrimination and/or prejudicial treatment. The homophobic behavior included: being the target of homophobic jokes (41 or 35%); being asked unwelcome questions about their sexuality (36 or 31%); being "outed" or having their sexuality disclosed (32 or 27%); being socially excluded (28 or 23%); being ridiculed (21 or 18%); being sexually harassed (19 or 16%); being threatened with physical violence (13 or 11%); being threatened with sexual violence (6 or 5%); and having property damaged (6 or 5%). Three participants experienced physical violence and one of these was also sexually assaulted.

> I experienced some overt discrimination including questioning about my sexuality, being outed, social exclusion, as well as over-supervision of my work and the threat of losing my job. My bosses saw the problem as my involvement with another worker rather than my sexuality but relationships between heterosexual employees weren't treated in this way. (25-year-old lesbian teacher)

> My office was trashed, and I had anonymous hate mail and phone calls. I have also been excluded from office functions. (39-year-old gay male academic)

The perpetrators of this behavior were most likely to be work colleagues employed either at a similar level or in a more senior position than the recipient of the homophobic behavior. For schoolteachers, the perpetrators of the homophobic behavior included students and their parents.

> I experienced student and parent harassment on the grounds of my perceived lesbianism. This involved accusations to both my immediate supervisor and the Deputy Principal. (42-year-old lesbian teacher)

> I experienced harassment from a small group of senior students who used to harass me by calling out "lesbian" when I walked past them, by writing lesbian on my property. They once threw an apple at me when I was on playground duty. I also had unwelcome questions from other students about my sexuality and insinuations that I looked like a man. (38-year-old lesbian teacher)

Many teachers, academics, or educators also experienced prejudicial treatment. The most frequent form was the undermining and sabotaging of work (26); unreasonable work expectations (18); limited opportunities for career development (18); threat of loss of promotion (16); and additional performance criteria (14). Twenty-one people stated they had been denied partner rights to superannuation, while 11 commented they had been denied entitlements available to heterosexual staff (e.g., parental leave, leave to care for an ill partner, compassionate leave).

> In 1995 my work was called into question. I was closely scrutinized and disciplined for no reason. I was treated differently by the principal and others. I ended up being forced out. I suffered emotionally and financially. I used to be out and confident and now I am not out and feel a loss of identity. (43-year-old lesbian teacher)

> I work in a Catholic school and I am not out. If I asked for my partner to be included in my superannuation I would out myself and that would be the end of my job. (29-year-old gay male teacher)

Some participants talked about how it was sometimes difficult to know whether they were being treated in a homophobic way. Others commented on the complexity of harassment and how it was not always possible to determine whether it was primarily homophobic or a combination of interacting factors.

> I was never really sure it was homophobic harassment. It was as much to do with me being a strong and assertive woman who would take him on. (45-year-old lesbian academic)

> It is difficult to say why I was discriminated against but I think it had more to do with being a woman than a lesbian and being an older and stroppy woman. (55-year-old lesbian teacher)

In or Out of the Closet

Some teachers, academics, and educators commented that they had not experienced homophobic behavior or prejudicial treatment because they had not been open about their sexuality.

> I was never discriminated against because I didn't come out till after I retired. No one knew I was gay. I lead a double life because my family still don't know. (69-year-old gay male retired teacher)

Only 8% (10) of teachers, academics, and educators were not open to anyone at work about their sexuality. Just under 35% (41) are out to everyone at work. This is a smaller proportion than in the complete survey, where 51% (448) of the participants identified they were out to everyone in their workplace. Teachers, academics, and educators were the occupational group in the research most likely to be selectively out (56% or 67) compared to 39% (347) in the complete survey. Many teachers, especially those employed in church schools, expressed concerns about being out and the risk this posed for their continuing employment.

> I'm not really out at work so I am in constant fear and anxiety of being found out and I would get the sack. It's a church school. (30-year-old lesbian teacher)

Some teachers commented on the negative consequences of being "found out" or presumed to be gay, lesbian, or transgender. Others commented that they were reticent about being open about their sexuality after experiencing homophobic harassment or discrimination in other schools, and for some these experiences took some time to overcome.

> After my previous experiences I was less prepared to be open about my sexuality. (53-year-old gay male teacher)

> I am fortunate to have a lesbian boss and co-workers. For the first time ever I feel safe at work. It took a long time to trust this. (52-year-old lesbian teacher)

A contextual factor that could have influenced school teachers' choices about being open about their sexuality was the "moral panic" that resulted from the Royal Commission into Police Corruption in the state of New South Wales between 1995 and 1997, which highlighted police protection of pedophiles. Some gay and lesbian teachers perceived that this reinforced the misconceptions that link homosexuality to pedophilia. This had a significant effect on many groups but particularly on gay men and lesbians who worked as teachers in schools (Ferfolja, forthcoming). However, the implications of this issue require further research. Many teachers, academics, and educators commented on the personal consequences for them of not feeling safe enough to be out about their sexual identity.

> I don't like not being open but if they knew I was gay I'd be out of a job. It is hard though to hide the most important part of your life and it causes fear and stress. (43-year-old gay male teacher)

> It takes a lot of energy to hide your sexuality and creates a lot of stress. (31-year-old lesbian teacher)

For some, being open about their sexuality was possible because they had supportive workplace colleagues, which meant they felt safe to be out.

> I don't want to hide what I do any more. Being open helped me to relate more honestly. (47-year-old gay male teacher)

Effects of Discrimination

All but three of the seventy-one teachers, academics, and educators who had experienced some form of discrimination commented that it had some negative effect on them or on their work performance. The most likely effect identified was an increase in their anxiety and stress levels (90% or 64). Many became depressed (80% or 57) and/or experienced a loss of confidence (63% or 45). Just under 62% (44) commented that they had become ill as a consequence of their treatment with just over 59% (41) commenting that it had a negative effect on their personal relationships. Thirteen (18%) commented that they had increased their drug and alcohol intake. Twelve (16%) commented that they had contemplated suicide and one person said he had attempted suicide. As a consequence of the ongoing harassment, 30 (42%) said they had sought counseling, and 24 (34%) had sought medical treatment.

> The constant stress had eroded my confidence and self esteem. I began to think about how I had contributed and began to blame myself for the situation. I know I shouldn't think like this but sometimes I just can't help it. (34-year-old gay male academic)

> I suffered a complete nervous breakdown. It made me depressed and I lost total confidence in my ability to do the job. I even thought about killing myself. (41-year-old lesbian teacher)

Many commented on the negative effects of either being exposed to, or being fearful of homophobic harassment at their work. Forty-two (59%) said it had resulted in them achieving less at work, 51 (72%) commented that they had considered resigning, 27 (38%) had resigned,

33 (46%) had taken sick leave, 35 (49%) had decided on a career change and 13 (18%) said they had been sacked.

> I worked for a religious school and experienced extreme and systematic discriminatory behavior, including being the target of homophobic jokes and remarks, being asked unwelcome questions, ridicule, social exclusion, threats of physical violence. I eventually resigned rather than seek sickness compensation, which they were refusing to give me. (28-year-old gay male teacher)

Some participants commented that the fear of becoming the target of harassment affected the way they behaved or what they had to do to be accepted.

> I had to work twice as hard building up positive relationships. (37-year-old lesbian academic)

> The same rules didn't apply to me as to the straight people. I had to be very careful about how I related to the kids. It was constraining sometimes. (29-year-old gay male teacher)

Many of the participants commented on the effect that the existence of homophobic behavior and harassment had in the creation of a negative culture in the workplace. For example, many of those who experienced being the target of homophobic jokes or being socially excluded, commented that while these types of homophobic behaviors may seem minimal, they nevertheless contributed to the creation of a workplace culture that was hostile and unsafe and where it was often necessary to be "on guard." For many this reinforced their difference in a negative way and created an atmosphere of intolerance. Others, however, viewed it differently; as one gay man said, "It was a blessed relief to be excluded." Likewise, some considered behavior such as social exclusion had no effect on their performance at work, while others considered it did have an effect on their work performance and their sense of self.

Action Taken Against the Homophobic Harassment and Treatment

While experiences of homophobic behavior, harassment, and unfair treatment were extensive, less than half (45% or 32) of the teachers, academics, and educators who experienced homophobic harassment or treatment chose to take action. Teachers, academics, and educators were nevertheless the occupational group most likely to take action. In the larger research project only 36% (192) of those who experienced discriminatory behavior or treatment took some form of action.

The most likely action taken was either to confront the offender or to discuss it with management or senior staff. Responses varied, and ranged from the harassment ceasing to the claim not being taken seriously by executive staff. Only two teachers sought advice or assistance from their union. Some commented that they did not consider that the union would act for them on an issue such as homophobic harassment as they saw the core business of unions as work conditions and salaries. Others commented on the homophobic treatment they had experienced within the union movement.

> The union was full of homophobes. Perpetrators are usually union members too and have "mates" in union positions. The union is only good for wages and other conditions. (36-year-old gay male teacher)

Positive Experiences

There were participants who identified positive experiences in their workplaces. Very often this was associated with their employers' (and senior staff) commitment to the promotion of diversity. In these situations, discrimination of any kind was not acceptable and this was reflected in the attitudes of staff.

> The university in which I work is tolerant of difference. This is one of the reasons I decided to come out when I moved here as I thought it was safe. All staff and students know me and that I am a lesbian and that my partner works here. (46-year-old lesbian academic)

> My current workplace has been a good experience and has improved my life and confidence outside work mainly because the boss who is a lesbian has made it clear to staff, students, and parents that the school does not tolerate homophobia. Staff support this and students are dealt with immediately and appropriately. For the first time in my working career I have not heard a single homophobic joke or assumption in staffrooms. (46-year-old lesbian teacher)

CONCLUSION

Employers and unions have responsibility and a duty of care to protect employees against discrimination of any kind. It is the employer's responsibility to ensure that employees are protected against homophobic harassment and prejudicial treatment. The creation of a safe, productive, and inclusive workplace is dependent upon employers creating a workplace environment where there are disincentives for perpetrating homophobic harassment and prejudicial treatment. Employers need to be active in challenging individual, institutional, and systemic discrimination in the workplace. While employers may not be actively reinforcing homophobic practices and behaviors, they can collude with these practices by not actively challenging them. The need for close examination of employment and workplace practices to ensure that people are all treated in a fair and just way is paramount. It is only by doing this and creating transparent policy, procedures, and practices that inclusive workplaces will be created.

REFERENCES

Anti-Discrimination Board of New South Wales. (1982). *Discrimination and homosexuality*. Sydney: Author.

Anti-Discrimination Board of New South Wales. (1990). *What is lesbian discrimination*? Sydney: Author.

Anti-Discrimination Board of New South Wales. (1992). *Discrimination–the other epidemic: Report of the inquiry into HIV and AIDS related discrimination*. Sydney: Author.

Ferfolja, T. (forthcoming). *Standing in the shadows: Lesbian teachers' experiences of silencing in New South Wales' high schools*. Unpublished doctoral thesis, University of New South Wales, Australia.

Irwin, J. (1999). *"The pink ceiling is too low" : Workplace experiences of lesbians, gay men and transgender people*. Report of a collaborative research project undertaken by the Australian Center for Lesbian and Gay Research and the New South Wales Gay and Lesbian Rights Lobby, Sydney: Australian Center for Lesbian and Gay Research, University of Sydney.

Gays and Lesbians Against Discrimination. (1994). *"Not a day goes by" : Report on the GLAD survey into discrimination and violence against lesbians and gay men in Victoria*. Melbourne: Author.

New South Wales Gay and Lesbian Rights Lobby. (1992). *The off our backs report*. Sydney: Author.

New South Wales Gay and Lesbian Rights Lobby. (1994). *The count & counter report*. Sydney: Author.

Heterosexual Attitudes to Homosexuality: Homophobia at a Rural Australian University

Max Hopwood
John Connors

SUMMARY. This study compared attitudes towards homosexuality of 164 students from two faculties at a rural Australian university. Eighty-two percent of participants were aged from 18-24 years, 65% percent of the sample were female with 58% of participants enrolled in a humanities course and 42% in a business course. A cross-sectional design using the Heterosexual Attitudes to Homosexuals (H.A.T.H.) and Fear of HIV/AIDS questionnaires found that for the total sample the major predictors of homophobia were fear of HIV/AIDS, gender, religiosity, and academic major. Business majors were significantly more homophobic than humanities majors. The findings imply that homophobia may be prevalent among university faculties and that staff and student programs need to be implemented to address homophobia, especially among business majors and lecturers. *[Article copies available for a fee from The Haworth Document Delivery Service: 1-800-HAWORTH. E-mail address: <getinfo@haworthpressinc.com> Website: <http://www.HaworthPress.com> © 2002 by The Haworth Press, Inc. All rights reserved.]*

Max Hopwood, BA (Hons), is affiliated with the National Centre in HIV Social Research, Faculty of Arts and Social Sciences, Level 2 Robert Webster Building, The University of New South Wales, Sydney NSW 2052 Australia (E-mail: m.hopwood@unsw.edu.au). John Connors, BA (First Class Hons), MA, Master of Letters, is affiliated with the School of Humanities & Social Sciences, Charles Sturt University, Locked Bag 678, Wagga Wagga NSW 2678, Australia (E-mail: jconnors@csu.edu.au).

[Haworth co-indexing entry note]: "Heterosexual Attitudes to Homosexuality: Homophobia at a Rural Australian University." Hopwood, Max, and John Connors. Co-published simultaneously in *Journal of Gay & Lesbian Social Services* (Harrington Park Press, an imprint of The Haworth Press, Inc.) Vol. 14, No. 2, 2002, pp. 79-94; and: *From Here to Diversity: The Social Impact of Lesbian and Gay Issues in Education in Australia and New Zealand* (ed: Kerry H. Robinson, Jude Irwin, and Tania Ferfolja) Harrington Park Press, an imprint of The Haworth Press, Inc., 2002, pp. 79-94. Single or multiple copies of this article are available for a fee from The Haworth Document Delivery Service [1-800-HAWORTH, 9:00 a.m. - 5:00 p.m. (EST). E-mail address: getinfo@haworthpressinc.com].

KEYWORDS. Homophobia, attitudes, university students, predictors, social identity, prejudice, faculty, homosexuality

INTRODUCTION

This study investigated homophobic attitudes among a sample of students identifying as heterosexual at a rural university campus in New South Wales. By utilizing theoretical discourse concerned with social identity and contact between social groups, predictors of homophobia and variations in prejudice as a function of academic major were highlighted. Religious, sociopolitical and gender-role identity have been implicated in previous studies of homophobia (Seltzer, 1992). Similarly, research has illustrated the importance of interaction between individuals and social groups for either confirming or disconfirming prejudices (Allport, 1958). Previous research has explored the processes involved in acquiring and maintaining prejudiced beliefs and this work underpins many recent investigations of attitudes to homosexuality (Allport, 1958; Argyle & Beit-Hallahmi, 1975; Kerlinger, 1984). In this present study, social identity theory and the contact hypothesis are posited as two significant and complementary theoretical explanations for negative attitudes towards lesbians and gay men.

SOCIAL IDENTITY: POLITICAL AND RELIGIOUS VALUES

Social identity theory involves three basic assumptions: people categorize others into in-groups and out-groups; people are motivated to strive for a positive self-concept and gain a sense of self-esteem by identifying with a particular in-group; and people's self-concept partly depends on how they evaluate their in-group compared to other groups (Sears, Peplau & Taylor, 1991). This theory describes people's desire to belong to a 'superior' group, and the psychological, social and material benefits obtained from such membership. By identifying with specific religious and sociopolitical groups and gender roles, in-group norms, values and beliefs provide a structure from which individuals view the 'other.'

While exceptions are apparent, it is generally accepted that people's social, political, and economic beliefs tend to be ideologically organized or patterned, and attitudes to minorities are included in this patterning. The prevailing view is that sociopolitical beliefs cluster into a basic bipolar left-right dimension, with one pole labeled liberalism and the other conservatism (Kerlinger, 1984). Generally it is assumed, for example, that racial tolerance, support for women's equality, and acceptance of homosexuality tend to be associated with liberalism rather than conservatism (Kerlinger, 1984). One theory of conservatism which illuminates the association between the Right and tendencies toward prejudice attitude formation is provided by Wilson (1973), who suggests that an individual's orientation to change is the organizing principle behind the ideological patterning of attitudes and beliefs evident in the liberal-conservative dimension. Negative reaction to change may stem from a personality trait that reflects a fear of uncertainty, and could explain a lesser willingness on the part of conservatives to accept people who are different (Kerlinger, 1984). Generally, research has supported the theorizing of ideological patterning into a Left and Right spectrum (see Bouton, Gallaher, Garlinghouse & Leal, 1989), indicating that political conservatives are usually more homophobic and fearful of HIV/AIDS than liberals.

Past research into the association between Judeo-Christian religious adherence and prejudiced attitudes found that church members are often more prejudiced than non-church members (Argyle & Beit-Hallahmi, 1975). Religiosity predicted ethical conservatism, which in turn predicted homophobia (Vander Stoep & Green, 1988). Religiosity and frequency of worship were positively correlated with prejudice towards gays and lesbians. Baptists and fundamentalist Christians were reported as more homophobic than Catholics, Jews, and many Protestant denominations, who in turn were more homophobic than those claiming no religious preference (Fisher, Derison, Polley & Cadman, 1994).

Generally, it appears that certain kinds of religious orientation, rather than religion as a whole, are instrumental in the formation of prejudiced attitudes (Allport, 1958). Argyle and Beit-Hallahmi (1975, p. 121) explain the relationship between religiosity and prejudice as a function of the churches' role in "unifying the community of believers around a consensus of values . . . [which involve] in-group and out-group distinctions and contribute to social divisions." While it is important to acknowledge the limitations of generalizing from demographic profiles and to be wary of forming assumptions about people's attitudes based solely on their group membership, the findings of the above research support the theory that politically conservative and religious people may be predisposed to homophobia.

Social identity theory has been used by Hamner (1992) to explain heterosexual male violence against gays and lesbians. That is, rather than being seen as a conflict between individuals, it is better understood as intergroup conflict. Heterosexuals use denigration to create a negative evaluation of homosexuals, which maintains a positive differentiation between the two groups and serves to bolster the heterosexuals' self-esteem. According to Herek (1992), anti-gay violence and homophobia must be understood within the context in which it occurs. That is, they are logical reactions and extensions of the heterosexism that pervades our culture. He defines heterosexism as an ideological system that "denies, denigrates and stigmatizes any non-heterosexual form of behavior, identity, relationship or community" (Herek, 1992, p. 89). As in racism and sexism, heterosexism is manifested in societal customs and institutions like religion and the law, and in individual attitudes and behavior.

Males who do not conform to stereotypical heterosexual masculine gender roles are usually viewed as more deviant and a more serious concern or threat to society than females who do not conform to their stereotypical feminine gender roles. This manifestation of heterosexism is supported by several studies that asked male and female undergraduates to assess a heterosexual, a gay man, and a lesbian. Gay men were rated significantly less favorably than the heterosexual, and lesbians were rated slightly less favorably than the heterosexual (McCreary, 1994; Page & Yee, 1985). These studies suggest that heterosexual males and females are more prejudiced toward gay males than lesbians.

Related to these findings is the consistent and empirically substantiated observation that heterosexual males are significantly more homophobic than heterosexual females (Chng & Moore, 1991; Piskur & Degalman, 1992).

THE CONTACT HYPOTHESIS

Gordon Allport's contact hypothesis (1958) suggests that to reduce prejudice between groups, interaction must occur and the contact must involve positive outcomes for all concerned. From past research, contact between heterosexuals and homosexuals appears to play a significant role in reducing homophobia (see Lance, 1987). Closeness with gays and lesbians is often the most significant discriminating variable with regard to attitudes toward homosexuals and people with HIV/AIDS. Respondents reporting high levels of contact with gays and lesbians were consistently less negative in their evaluation of homosexuals than those reporting low or no contact (Grieger &

Ponterotto, 1988). Respondents who knew gays and lesbians and cited them as close friends were better informed about HIV/AIDS and subsequently less fearful of the disease, and did not hold punitive views of people living with the condition (Noble, Kippax & Crawford, 1995).

Research into attitudes concerning HIV/AIDS suggests that people with a better knowledge of the condition are less fearful of it than those with a poorer knowledge (Connors & Heaven, 1995). A relationship between fear of HIV/AIDS and homophobic attitudes has been reported in a number of studies. Religious and political conservatives were generally more fearful of HIV/AIDS and more homophobic than liberals, and frequency of church attendance correlated with both fear of HIV/AIDS and homophobia (Bouton et al., 1989). A correlation between males' fear of HIV/AIDS and fear of homosexuality is evident in a number of US studies (Kunkel & Temple, 1992; McDevitt, Sheehan, Lennon & Ambrosio, 1990).

Finally, among subjects who displayed a moderate knowledge of the prevalence of HIV/AIDS, high risk practices, modes of transmission and symptoms, those who were least fearful of contracting the condition were also the most accepting of gay men. Generally, it appears that a low knowledge of HIV/AIDS correlates with a higher fear of HIV/AIDS, which correlates with a higher level of homophobia.

ACADEMIC MAJOR AND HOMOPHOBIA

Prejudiced attitudes existing among broader social demographic groups may be reflected in university students' academic major. Identification with specific religious and sociopolitical group and gender role norms is likely to vary according to academic major. Larsen, Reed, and Hoffman (1980) cite research that suggests differing levels of anti-gay sentiment are evident in students from different university faculties. Specifically, business majors were cited as less tolerant than other student groups. Similar findings were published by Bogardus as early as 1925, where he reported businessmen were less tolerant of members from various "races" than was the case for teachers. Larsen, Reed, and Hoffman (1980) suggest business majors may be more inclined to be prejudiced, because students who seek a career in business may come from families and social environments that promote competition as positive, and where success is defined as the accumulation of money and status. Competitive people often need to satisfy their esteem needs by placing themselves above others, and it is partly these needs for high esteem that determine a business major's attitudes towards others. Larson et al. (1980) cite links between business-oriented people and traits of conventionalism, aggression, and toughness, which are synonymous with an "authoritarian" personality. The authoritarian personality is sometimes evident in those identifying as religious and politically conservative, and these people are often negative in their evaluations of gays and lesbians. In sum, the business majors' competitive ideology and esteem needs, coupled with an affinity with authoritarian traits, may result in some of these students being less tolerant individuals and therefore more homophobic.

Many of the studies cited above report on urban American attitudes to homosexuality. Comparatively little research on this issue has been conducted in Australia, especially in a rural context. Although cultural similarities between the United States and Australia are evident, the experience of living in rural New South Wales, Australia, presents unique circumstances. The sample for this study was drawn from students attending a regional university in South-Western New South Wales. This university is situated outside a city of sixty thousand people located approximately four hundred fifty kilometers from Sydney. The region is a fertile agricultural area and agriculture is pivotal to the cultural landscape. The local business sector comprises many farm-associated industries. Most students attending the university are from surrounding local districts and nearby areas of southern and western New South Wales. Prompted by this previous and largely U.S. research, rural Australian heterosexual students' gender, religiosity, political orientation, fear of HIV/AIDS, and level of contact with gays and lesbians were examined to reveal their independent influences in determining homophobic attitudes.

The first hypothesis tested stated that religious and politically conservative males with a fear of HIV/AIDS and no contact with homosexuals were most likely to be homophobic. In addition, this study looked for differences in attitudes to homosexuality and HIV/AIDS between business and humanities undergraduates. The second hypothesis stated that business majors would reveal higher levels of homophobia than would humanities majors.

METHOD

Participants

The sample consisted of 164 first-year undergraduate students from a rural university in South-Western New South Wales. Ninety-six students were studying humanities courses and 68 students were from the Faculty of Business. Subjects' age ranged between 18 to 44 years with 82% being in the 18 to 24 year age group. The total sample consisted of 65% females and 35% males from a variety of ethnic backgrounds, with the majority being Caucasian.

Materials and Procedure

All participants were required to complete an anonymous three-part questionnaire. Part One contained the Heterosexual Attitudes to Homosexuals (H.A.T.H.) questionnaire by Larsen, Reed, and Hoffman (1980). Examples of items contained in part one of the scale are: "I enjoy the company of homosexuals," "Homosexuality is immoral," and "Homosexuality should be given social equality."

Part Two of the questionnaire enquired into participants' fear of HIV/AIDS using the Fear of AIDS scale by Bouton, Gallaher, Garlinghouse, Leal, Rosenstein, and Young (1987). Examples of items contained in this scale are: "I would object to sending my non-infected child to a school which had a child who has HIV/AIDS," and "If I found out that my lover had HIV/AIDS I would still have sex with him/her."

Part Three of the questionnaire measured a range of demographic variables. It included several questions designed to establish the participants' religiousness and political orientation. The items surveying religiousness asked: "How often do you attend church?" and "How much value do you attach to your religiosity?" An item surveying political orientation asked: "Who are you most likely to vote for in a general election?" Part Three also measured the participants' past or present contact with people known to them to be gay or lesbian. Finally, participants were asked to identify themselves as heterosexual, bisexual, homosexual, or other, and to state their gender.

RESULTS

Chi-square analyses of the demographic variables were performed to ensure both samples were homogeneous. The only significant difference between the two groups was gender (χ^2 (1) = 10.88, p = .000), due to a larger proportion of females amongst the humanities majors. Humanities majors indicate higher levels of current contact with gays and lesbians; however, this narrowly fails to reach significance (χ^2 (2) = 5.75, p = .056).

Regarding attitudes to gays and lesbians, the two means for scores on the H.A.T.H. reveal a significant difference between business majors (M = 53.93) and humanities majors (M = 43.77), (t (162) = 3.85, p < .01), with the higher mean for business majors indicating higher homophobia. Similarly, when the two means for the Fear of HIV/AIDS scale are compared, a significant difference is evident with business majors (M = 39.65) reporting a greater fear of HIV/AIDS than did humanities majors (36.45) (t (162) = 2.67, p < .01).

A review of the Pearson correlations among the variables for the total sample shows that all nine variables correlate significantly with homophobia: respondents reporting high levels of homophobia are politically conservative (r = .22, p < .01), are more likely to come from the business faculty (r = .29, p < .01) and view religion as very important (r = .35, p < .01). Regular church attendance is associated with higher homophobia scores (r = .17, p < .05). Scores on the two scales H.A.T.H. and Fear of HIV/AIDS are significantly correlated (r = .64, p < .01), suggesting a strong correlation between respondents' homophobia level and their fear of HIV/AIDS. Those respondents reporting either no current contact or who are unsure as to whether they currently have contact with homosexuals reveal higher levels of homophobia than those citing current contact (r = .25, p < .01). Respondents reporting either no previous contact or uncertainty as to whether they have had previous contact reveal higher levels of homophobia (r = .26, p < .01). Finally, males are associated with higher homophobia levels more than females (r = .28, p < .01).

REGRESSING HOMOPHOBIA

To explore the hypothesis that gender, political orientation, religiosity, fear of HIV/AIDS, and contact with gays and lesbians would predict homophobia, a stepwise multiple regression analysis was performed using the total sample. The independent variable Fear of HIV/AIDS is a significant predictor of homophobia (F (1,162) = 111.06, p = .0000) and accounts for nearly 41% of the variation in scores. Gender is a significant predictor of attitudes to homosexuality (F (2,161) = 65.20, p = .0007) and contributes approximately 4% to the explained variance. Importance of religion is a predictor of homophobia (F (3, 160) = 52.87, p = .0001) and contributes a further 5% to the explained variance. Academic major is also a predictor of homophobia (F (4, 159) = 42.04, p = .0228) contributing 1.6% to the explained variance. The four independent variables (Fear of HIV/AIDS, gender, importance of religion, and academic major) together account for 51.4% of the explained variance in scores on the H.A.T.H. scale. Political orientation narrowly missed out on being included in the regression equation.

REGRESSING HOMOPHOBIA FROM SEPARATE SUBSAMPLES

Two further stepwise multiple regression analyses were performed to identify the variables that predict homophobia relative to each subsample. Business majors report Fear of HIV/AIDS as the most significant predictor of negative attitudes to homosexuality (F (1,66) = 54.07, p = .0000), and this variable accounts for 45% of the explained variation in scores. Political Orientation is a significant predictor of homophobia (F (2,65) = 32.05, p = .0173), contributing a further 4.7% to the explained variance. Finally, Current Contact with homosexuals is a significant predictor of homophobia (F (3,64) = 24.73, p = .0124), accounting for 4% of the explained variance. Together, Fear of HIV/AIDS, Political Orientation, and Current Contact with homosexuals account for 53.7% of the explained variation in scores for the business majors.

With regard to the humanities majors, Fear of HIV/AIDS is the most significant predictor of attitudes to homosexuality (F (1,94) = 46.01, p = .0000), and accounts for nearly 33% of the explained variation in scores. The importance of religion is a significant predictor of homophobia (F (2,93) = 31.98, p = .0007) and contributes 7.8% to the explained variance. Having previous contact with homosexuals is a significant predictor of homophobia in this sample (F (3,92) = 24.48, p = .0159), and accounts for a further 3.6% of the explained variation in scores. Finally, gender is a significant predictor of homophobia (F (4,91) = 20.44, p = .0268) and contributes 3% to the explained variance. In total, the variables Fear of HIV/AIDS, Previous Contact, Gender, and Religiosity are the significant predictors of homophobia for the humanities majors and together account for 47% of the explained variation in scores on the H.A.T.H.

DISCUSSION

In sum, Fear of HIV/AIDS, Gender, Religiosity, Academic Major, Political Orientation, and Previous and Current Contact were all significant predictors of attitudes to homosexuals in the context of this sample of undergraduate students. However, the variable Fear of HIV/AIDS contributed greatly to negative attitudes to homosexuals and the other variables, although significant, contributed only a relatively small degree to the variation in scores on the homophobia scale. This study's findings were congruent with the statement of hypotheses.

FEAR OF HIV/AIDS

The most powerful predictor of homophobia was a respondent's fear of HIV/AIDS. The correlation between fear of HIV/AIDS and homophobia in this study was 0.64 for the total sample, indicating a very strong association between the variables. This prompts the question, is fear of HIV/AIDS little more than an expression of homophobia? Previous research by Bouton, Gallaher, Garlinghouse, Leal, Rosenstein, and Young (1987) analyzing the factors in the Fear of HIV/AIDS scale and a similar homophobia scale to the H.A.T.H. suggested that the two scales were relatively independent of each other and did not represent a single underlying attitude. No evidence was reported to suggest that fear of HIV/AIDS is just another way of expressing homophobia. A later study by Bouton et al. (1989) supported these earlier findings, and it was suggested that the strong association between fear of HIV/AIDS scores and homophobia scores resulted from respondents' general concern with issues of public health. The availability heuristic, however, could explain the high correlations, as at the time of these studies media attention was focused on the link between HIV/AIDS and gay communities, and in the minds of the population the two issues were synonymous.

Bouton et al. (1989) and Kunkel and Temple (1992) have predicted that with the increased reporting of HIV/AIDS in the heterosexual population, and as people from a variety of backgrounds contract the virus, then the strength of the association between AIDS and homosexuality, as perceived by the public, will weaken. Bouton et al. (1987) reported a correlation of 0.55 between fear of HIV/AIDS and homophobia, whereas Kunkel and Temple (1992), using similar scales five years later, reported a decrease in the correlation to 0.48. The correlation of 0.64

between fear of HIV/AIDS and homophobia reported in the present study goes against the hypothesized trend. However, this could be explained by differences between the samples obtained. Indeed, the decrease in reported correlations of the two American studies cited could also be due to sampling differences.

The high correlation between fear of HIV/AIDS and homophobia scores would suggest that for this sample fear of HIV/AIDS may actually be an expression of homophobia. In Australia today, a strong association between HIV/AIDS and gay lifestyle persists in the minds of the general population, reinforced by epidemiological figures showing rates of recent HIV infection in developed countries remaining higher for gay men than for heterosexuals. Media images of recent issues, such as combination therapies for the treatment of HIV, focus on gay men in their story presentations. File footage from past Sydney Gay and Lesbian Mardi Gras parades and parties often feature as a backdrop to news items on HIV vaccine trials, providing a subtext suggesting that the virus is predominantly a gay man's issue. Perhaps not surprising then, in the present study the pattern of correlations between the demographic variables and scores on the Fear of HIV/AIDS scale was similar to those found to be associated with homophobia. For example, when viewing the total sample, business majors report being both more fearful of HIV/AIDS and homophobic than humanities majors. For this sample, AIDS and homosexuality may predominantly represent two sides of the one coin.

Gender

In many previous studies of homophobia, males are often found to exhibit more negative attitudes to homosexuality than females. In this study, being male was a predictor of homophobia for the total sample and also the humanities subsample. The culture of heterosexual masculinity is a defining element of the Australian male. "Maleness" is a highly prized commodity in rural Australia (Roberts, 1995), and many heterosexually identified males may feel compelled to raise barriers between themselves and gay men in order to protect their "prize." In the presence of strong homosocial relationships, that is, the mateship and camaraderie expressed by heterosexual men through, for example, their common interests in sports, expressions of homophobic sentiment may serve to delineate the fragile boundary between homosociality and homosexuality, and therefore contribute to keeping men sexually apart (Sedgwick, 1985). Homophobia may be used as an intervention into all male behavior; an adaptive means of maintaining heterosexuality in contexts where homosexual relations may easily develop and "disrupt" the order of power relationships and heterosexual male sex-role norms.

Women are consistently less homophobic than men across most studies. Explanation is likely to be multi-factorial; however, women's interpretation of a violation of sex-role norms may be significant. Fundamental to this reading is feminism's interrogation of the proscriptive sex-role play that defines heteronormative notions of gender. The patriarchal model of masculinity and femininity has been deconstructed to reveal its implicit messages of social power and powerlessness. The profile that has emerged of an intellectually and financially independent woman reflects the achievements of twentieth-century feminism to reconfigure the public-private sphere dichotomy. Many women appreciate the value of questioning assumptions inherent to the patriarchal model of gender relations. Similarly, many women may positively view, for example, the gay man who interrogates, and violates, his sex-role norm. His nonadherence to and reconfiguring of "vital" indicators of masculinity may reinforce expression of a widespread gendered unhappiness with the expectations of heterosexism. Conversely, men, who historically have so much invested in the patriarchal model of masculine power, find sex-role violations an affront and threat to men's social-power positioning.

Religiosity

Social identity theory may give clues to why some religious individuals tend to be more homophobic than nonreligious people. With the decline in Australia of the importance and power of religion in daily life, the self-esteem of some believers may have been compromised. As the theory predicts, to rebuild and preserve self-esteem religious advocates must motivate in-group favoritism, while simultaneously increasing prejudice towards outgroups. Homosexuals are a traditional social outgroup with an inferior status to the established authority of the church, and therefore represent a relevant focus for the expression of prejudiced attitudes. Perhaps the incidence of homophobic sentiment expressed by some religious advocates in this predominantly youthful sample reflects the unease that accompanies being marginalized, and represents an attempt to maintain self-esteem at a time in one's life when belonging to a group and being accepted by one's peers is salient. In this context, homophobia can be viewed as an adaptive response to a threat, that is, the decline in the social importance of religion.

Academic Major as a Predictor of Homophobia

Academic major was a significant predictor of homophobia. There were also different predictors of homophobia between the two faculty groups. After fear of HIV/AIDS, gender, importance of religion, and previous contact with gays and lesbians predicted homophobia for the humanities subsample. Fear of HIV/AIDS, political orientation, and current contact with gays and lesbians were the variables predicting homophobia for the business subsample. While having contact with gays and lesbians predicted homophobia in both subsamples, overall this variable did not prove to contribute significantly to variation in attitudes to homosexuality. The business subsample indicates significantly higher levels of homophobia and fear of HIV/AIDS than the humanities subsample. This may be partly due to the influence of more male respondents.

CHALLENGING HOMOPHOBIA: IMPLICATIONS FOR EDUCATION

While comprehensive social change in attitudes to homosexuality is incremental, major individual shifts in opinion do sometimes occur more rapidly. Some early social psychological research (see Newcomb, 1943) suggests that students reassess their attitudes in relation to social issues under specific circumstances. Newcomb's (1943) study of students' political attitudes found that through exposure to liberal faculty staff, conservative students' attitudes changed during their time at college and became more liberal. Newcomb's study illustrates the effects of teachers' attitudes on students and the capacity for education to promote a reassessment of students' values and beliefs originally acquired from their families.

This has implications for teacher training and practice with regard to reducing homophobia among students. For university business majors' attitudes to change, the attitudes of business faculty lecturers and tutors must also be addressed. Students from a conservative rural background entering a tertiary business faculty may modify their negative attitudes to marginalized social groups if tolerance and acceptance of minority groups and cultural diversity is evident among their lecturers. However, lecturers in business studies are likely to be immersed in a similar social milieu to their protégés and therefore likely to exhibit similar heterosexist and homophobic attitudes. Attempting to overcome "the ignorance, complacency, or anti-homosexual prejudice of many educators" is described by Van dc Ven (1996, p. 194) as a useful starting point to address the homophobic sentiments of students. Informal discussion, conferences, staff meetings, and professional workshops are posited as some methods by which educators' awareness of homosexuality may be raised and attitudes changed (Van de Ven, 1996). An emphasis on examining educators' attitudes to homosexuality, rather than simply imparting knowledge, should form the basis of training of educational personnel (Fassinger, 1993).

In relation to business majors, where research indicates a faculty propensity for prejudiced attitudes, specifically tailored anti-homophobia teaching strategies need to be designed and modules introduced in the curriculum (Van de Ven, 1996). Such strategies may address faculty-specific stereotyping and prejudice by facilitating a targeted response to anti-homosexual sentiment that takes into account the educational context.

It is beyond the scope of this study to draw any conclusions with regard to the social implications for gay men and lesbians who work in or deal with the business sector. While findings from this study imply that business cultures are homophobic towards gays and lesbians, inferences need to be cautious, particularly as the international business environment becomes increasingly dynamic and diverse. Research comparing corporate cultures with other work environments would provide evidence as to whether the findings of this study resonate with the experiences of gay and lesbians in the business workplace.

CONCLUSION

What emerges from the analysis of the data for this sample is a profile of the homophobic individual as fearful of HIV/AIDS, male, a student of Business Studies, religious, and having no previous or current contact with homosexuals. This profile, with minor variation, has been drawn previously over the past decade in the research into anti-gay sentiment. It needs to be restated that there are limitations in generalizing from demographic profiles and that individual group members who behave contrary to group norms are evident among the research literature. However, the present study does reinforce the findings from previous research that specific demographic groups can be identified as more prejudiced than others. Individuals are homophobic not only because of idiosyncratic personality traits, but also because they belong to and identify with certain social groups that produce, perpetuate, and reinforce their individual prejudices (Noble, Kippax & Crawford, 1995). This highlights the social nature of homophobia, that is, the institutions and structures within society where anti-gay sentiment exists largely unchallenged. Efforts to reduce homophobia have attempted to reduce ignorance of homosexuality, for example, through community-based education programs aimed at demystifying gay and lesbian relationships. However, the implications of these findings, and those from previous studies, suggest that such a course of action may only have limited success in reducing negative attitudes to homosexuality. The demographic groups where homophobia is the norm are unlikely to alter their negative attitudes, if those very attitudes serve a purpose. If homophobia helps males, for example, to define and assert their heterosexual masculinity, then it would require a major social change to concepts of 'maleness' before homophobia could be reduced. Homophobia appears to serve a socially adaptive function for certain groups and a positive change in attitudes towards gays and lesbians is likely to be slow.

REFERENCES

Allport, G.W. (1958). *The nature of prejudice*. New York: Doubleday Anchor.

Argyle, M., & Beit-Hallahmi, B. (1975). *The social psychology of religion*. London: Routledge and Kegan Paul.

Bogardus, E. S. (1925). Measuring social distances. *Journal of Applied Sociology, 9*, 216-226.

Bouton, R.A., Gallaher, P.E., Garlinghouse, P.A., & Leal, T. (1989). Demographic variables associated with fear of AIDS and homophobia. *Journal of Applied Social Psychology, 19*, 885-901.

Bouton, R.A., Gallaher, P.E., Garlinghouse, P.A., Leal, T., Rosenstein, L.D., & Young, R.K. (1987). Scales for measuring fear of AIDS and homophobia. *Journal of Personality Assessment, 51*, 606-614.

Chng, C.L., & Moore, A. (1991). Can attitudes of college students towards AIDS and homosexuality be changed in six weeks? The effects of a gay panel. *Health Values: Health Behavior, Education and Promotion, 15*, 41-49.

Connors, J., & Heaven, P. (1995). Health beliefs and attitudes towards people living with HIV/AIDS. *Journal of Applied Social Psychology, 25*, 922-931.

Fassinger, R.E. (1993). And gladly teach: Lesbian and gay issues in education. In L. Diamont (Ed.), *Homosexual issues in the workplace* (pp. 119-142). Washington DC: Taylor and Francis.

Fisher, R.D., Derison, D., Polley, C.F., & Cadman, J. (1994). Religiousness, religious orientation and attitudes towards gays and lesbians. *Journal of Applied Social Psychology, 24*, 614-630.

Grieger, I., & Ponterotto, J.G. (1988). Students' knowledge of AIDS and their attitudes towards gays and lesbians. *Journal of College Student Development, 29*, 415-422.

Hamner, K.M. (1992). Gay bashing: A social identity analysis of violence against lesbians and gay men. In G.M. Herek & K.T. Berrill (Eds.), *Hate crimes: Confronting violence against lesbians and gay men* (pp. 179-190). Newbury Park: Sage.

Herek, G.M. (1992). The social context of hate crimes: Notes on cultural heterosexism. In G.M. Herek & K.T. Berrill (Eds.), *Hate crimes: Confronting violence against lesbians and gay men* (pp. 89-104). Newbury Park: Sage.

Kerlinger, F.N. (1984). *Liberalism and conservatism: The nature and structure of social attitudes*. New Jersey: Lawrence Erlbaum.

Kunkel, L.E., & Temple, L.L. (1992). Attitudes towards AIDS and homosexuals: Gender, marital status and religion. *Journal of Applied Social Psychology, 22*, 1030-1040.

Lance, L.M. (1987). The effects of interaction with gay persons on attitudes towards homosexuality. *Human Relations, 40*, 329-336.

Larsen, K.S., Reed, M., & Hoffman, S. (1980). Attitudes of heterosexuals toward homosexuality: A Likert-type scale and construct validity. *The Journal of Sex Research, 16*, 245-257.

McCreary, D.R. (1994). The male role and avoiding femininity. *Sex Roles, 31*, 517-531.

McDevitt, T.M., Sheehan, E.P., Lennon, R., & Ambrosio, A.L. (1990). Correlates of attitudes towards AIDS. *Journal of Social Psychology, 130*, 699-701.

Newcomb, T. (1943). *Personality and social change*. New York: Dryden.

Noble, J., Kippax S., & Crawford, J. (1995). Some demographic correlates of HIV/AIDS related discrimination. *Australian Journal of Social Issues, 30*, 310-325.

Page, S., & Yee, M. (1985). Conception of male and female homosexual stereotypes among university undergraduates. *Journal of Homosexuality, 12*, 109-118.

Piskur, J., & Degelman, D. (1992). Effect of reading a summary of research about biological bases of homosexual orientation on attitudes toward homosexuals. *Psychological Reports, 71*, 1219-1225.

Roberts, R. (1995). A "fair go for all?" Discrimination and the experiences of some men who have sex with men in the bush. In P. Share (Ed.), *Communication and Culture in Rural Areas* (pp. 151-174). Wagga Wagga: Centre for Rural Social Research, Charles Sturt University.

Sears, D.O., Peplau, L.A., & Taylor, S.E. (1991). *Social psychology* (7th ed.). New Jersey: Englewood Cliffs, Prentice Hall.

Sedgwick, E. (1985). *Between men: English literature and male homosocial desire*. New York: Columbia University Press.

Seltzer, R. (1992). The social location of those holding anti-homosexual attitudes. *Sex Roles, 26*, 391-398.

Vander Stoep, S.W., & Green, C. (1988). Religiosity and homonegativism: A path-analytic study. *Basic and Applied Social Psychology, 9*, 135-147.

Van de Ven, P. (1996). Combating heterosexism in schools: Beyond short courses. In L. Laskey & C. Beavis (Eds.), *Schooling and sexualities: Teaching for a positive sexuality* (pp. 187-199). Victoria: Deakin University for Education and Change.

Wilson, G. (Ed.). (1973). *The psychology of conservatism*. London: Academic Press.

Psychiatric Disorder or Straight Prejudice? The Role of Education in Overcoming Homophobia

Mairwen K. Jones
Gerard Sullivan

SUMMARY. While once *homosexuality* was considered a psychiatric disorder, this article examines the extent to which *homophobia* (antihomosexual behavior) may be regarded as a psychiatric disorder by considering whether it represents a phobic disorder or a prejudice. The implications of this classification for treatment and the role of education in overcoming antihomosexual behavior are addressed. *[Article copies available for a fee from The Haworth Document Delivery Service: 1-800-HAWORTH. E-mail address: <getinfo@haworthpressinc.com> Website: <http://www.HaworthPress.com> © 2002 by The Haworth Press, Inc. All rights reserved.]*

KEYWORDS. Homosexuality, homophobia, prejudice, phobia, education, discrimination, antihomosexual

---

Mairwen K. Jones, PhD, is affiliated with the School of Behavioural and Community Health Sciences, Faculty of Health Sciences, Cumberland Campus, University of Sydney, PO Box 170, Lidcombe, 1825, New South Wales, Australia (E-mail: M.Jones@cchs.usyd.edu.au). Gerard Sullivan, PhD, is Associate Professor, Faculty of Education, University of Sydney, NSW 2006, Australia (E-mail: g.sullivan@edfac.usyd.edu.au).

[Haworth co-indexing entry note]: "Psychiatric Disorder or Straight Prejudice? The Role of Education in Overcoming Homophobia." Jones, Mairwen K., and Gerard Sullivan. Co-published simultaneously in *Journal of Gay & Lesbian Social Services* (Harrington Park Press, an imprint of The Haworth Press, Inc.) Vol. 14, No. 2, 2002, pp. 95-105; and: *From Here to Diversity: The Social Impact of Lesbian and Gay Issues in Education in Australia and New Zealand* (ed: Kerry H. Robinson, Jude Irwin, and Tania Ferfolja) Harrington Park Press, an imprint of The Haworth Press, Inc., 2002, pp. 95-105. Single or multiple copies of this article are available for a fee from The Haworth Document Delivery Service [1-800-HAWORTH, 9:00 a.m. - 5:00 p.m. (EST). E-mail address: getinfo@haworthpressinc.com].

Prior to the 1970s, homosexuality was generally considered to be indicative of psychiatric pathology. Medical theories pathologized lesbians and gay men as sick, aggressive, tragically unhappy, and self-destructive (Sullivan, 2000; Wilbur, 1965). Treatments, which were often invasive and exploitative, were designed to change homosexual orientation. These treatments included psychiatric institutionalization, electroshock treatment, hormonal injections, and psychotherapy (Council on Scientific Affairs, 1987). With the rise of the gay rights movement in the 1970s, challenges were forthcoming to the diagnosis of homosexuality as a psychiatric disorder. There was resentment at the pathologizing of what was argued to be a legitimate alternative expression of human sexuality. Pressure began to be applied to remove it as a diagnostic category (Sullivan, 1987; Sullivan & Waite, 1997). In 1973, the Board of Trustees of the American Psychiatric Association decided to remove homosexuality per se from the Diagnostic and Statistical Manual of Mental Disorders (DSM) (Bayer, 1981). The third edition of DSM refers instead to ego-dystonic homosexuality, but clearly states that "homosexuality that is ego-syntonic is not classified as a mental disorder" (American Psychiatric Association, 1980, p. 282).

More recently, the spotlight has turned to examining antihomosexual behavior and the extent to which it can be considered a pathological condition. Consideration is now being given to developing evidence that homophobia may deserve a place in the DSM. This article examines the extent to which homophobia shares common features with other phobic disorders. Negative attitudes and behaviors towards homosexuals constitute a serious problem in many societies (e.g., Cunneen, Fraser & Tomsen 1997; Herek, 1989). Individuals who are perceived to be lesbian or gay may be the target of a range of negative reactions. These include physical or verbal violence and exclusion from adequate service provision, including health care. A better understanding of the nature of homophobia will enable the development of effective interventions to reduce this phenomenon and thus improve the quality of life of many individuals in our society.

The term homophobia was conceived by Weinberg in 1967 and referred to the dread of being in close quarters with homosexuals (Weinberg, 1972). While dread is defined in the Oxford English Dictionary as "great fear" (Sykes, 1976), the word homophobia has been widely used to refer to a range of responses to homosexuals, not all of which specifically relate to fear. As such, homophobia is commonly used to indicate any negative thoughts, feelings or behaviors towards those who are sexually attracted to persons of their own sex.

Since modern usage of the word "homophobia" is not always consistent with its original meaning, it has been argued that a term with broader applicability should be used. Hudson and Ricketts (1980) introduced the term homonegativism to refer to a multidimensional set of antihomosexual responses. One dimension includes "the responses of fear, disgust, anger, discomfort and aversion that individuals experience in dealing with gay people" (Hudson & Ricketts, 1980, p. 358). This dimension is largely equivalent to Weinberg's (1972) definition for homophobia.

While it has been suggested that not all antihomosexual responses involve fear, it is possible that some reactions to homosexual stimuli may be correctly identified as phobic. The word "phobia" refers to an irrational or excessive fear resulting in conscious avoidance of a specific feared object, activity, or situation (Kaplan & Sadock, 1988). Common phobic stimuli include spiders, heights, blood, injury, and enclosed environments (American Psychiatric Association, 1994) but can also include a variety of other objects and situations (such as balloons and crowds). Given the diversity of stimuli that may provoke fear, it is not inconceivable that *some* individuals may actually experience a phobic reaction to homosexuals.

Knowledge of the nature, etiology, and treatment of phobic disorders has advanced considerably in recent years. It would be useful to know the extent to which we can apply this information to homophobia. Unfortunately, there is a paucity of research investigating the nature of homophobia. Additionally, the investigations conducted to date assessing the existence of a true phobic response are not adequate. While homophobia is not a medically recognized phobia (Bhugra, 1987), some responses exhibited by homophobic individuals do appear analogous to those of phobic individuals when confronted with fear relevant stimuli. This can be seen in the verbal reactions reported from a study conducted by Van de Ven (1995a).

RESEARCH STUDIES

Using a series of structured questions, Van de Ven (1995a) assessed attitudes towards lesbians and gay males. Reactions identified from the 31 participants' responses included discomfort, disgust, and revulsion. When asked why some young people do not harass or bash gay males or lesbians, two participants reasoned that it was because harassing or bashing would entail "getting too close for comfort." One participant commented that the reason his friends were not violent towards gay people was "Because they're too scared to go next to them, just too scared to do it . . ." (p. 32). This response could be interpreted as equivalent to that of a phobic individual who experiences fear of potential contact and subsequent avoidance of the phobic stimulus.

Logan (1996) indicated that there are at least two distinct forms of homophobia, one associated with prejudice, and the other resembling recognized phobic reactions. Logan (1996) identified a small group of homophobics who satisfied clinical criteria for specific phobia, while the majority of antihomosexual responses were categorized as reflecting prejudice rather than fear. Similarities between homophobia and phobic disorders have been identified by several authors. While those with phobias commonly view their feared stimulus as potentially dangerous and threatening, males who hold negative attitudes about male homosexuality similarly perceive male homosexuals to be threatening and anxiety provoking (Serdahely & Ziemba, 1984). While Logan's (1996) phobic subgroup was relatively small (nine of 384 students), the prevalence of phobia may have been underestimated because Logan did not include items associated with a disgust reaction, such as "homosexuality is disgusting." The disgust response is fundamental to some phobic disorders (e.g., blood, injection, and injury phobias [Ost, Sterner & Lindahl, 1984]); therefore, we cannot exclude the possibility that a disgust reaction may underlie some homophobic responses. Finally, the findings would have been strengthened if the nine "phobic" participants had taken part in a clinical interview establishing definitive diagnosis for specific phobia.

Despite these limitations, the important finding of this study is that in some individuals a true phobic response appears to have been identified. The idea that negative attitudes toward male homosexuality are associated with fear has led researchers and the lay public to label homonegative attitudes as "homophobic" (Herek, 1984; Morin & Garfinkle, 1978; Weinberg, 1972). Since the majority of antihomosexual responses in Logan's (1996) study were categorized as prejudice, it was suggested that the term homophobia in its general usage is a misnomer. Instead, it should only be used in reference to individuals who experience a genuine phobic response to homosexuals.

In Logan's (1996) study, direct physiological or behavioral measures were not obtained. When investigating homophobia, measures assessing beliefs, thoughts, or ideas about homosexual-related stimuli have been commonly employed. While cognitive attitudes have therefore been the target of most homophobia research to date, the inadequacy of empirical work examining affective and behavioral responses to homosexuality has been noted (e.g., Van de Ven, 1994). Assessment of the behavioral domain is currently limited to interpersonal distance or chair placement studies (see below), with only one study directly assessing affective responses to homosexual stimuli.

Shields and Harriman (1984) measured the cardiac response of males with high or low negative attitudes toward male homosexuals while they watched slides of landscapes and slides depicting explicit male-to-male sexual activity. They hypothesized that if high homonegative males were actually homophobic they would exhibit a phobic response as evidenced by heart rate acceleration to slides of male-male sexual activity and deceleration to all other slide types. Their research provided some evidence consistent with this hypothesis, confirming the existence of the phobic type of heart rate acceleratory pattern among some, but not all, high homonegative males.

While this is the first study to directly examine the affective domain of homophobia and its equivalence to other phobias, there are significant potential confounds to consider when interpreting these findings. First, it is possible that the heart rate acceleration recorded in some participants was due to anger or sexual arousal rather than arousal due to fear. Adams, Wright, and Lohr (1996) suggest that sexual arousal may have contributed to the heart rate acceleration observed by Shields and Harriman (1984). When Adams, Wright, and Lohr (1996) exposed 35 homophobic and 29 nonhomophobic men to male homosexual stimuli, only the homophobic men were found to have an increase in penile circumference. The researchers concluded that homophobia may be associated with homosexual arousal.

An additional limitation to Shields and Harriman's (1984) pilot study was the small sample size. There were only five high-scoring and five low-scoring homonegative participants in the study. Finally, the fact that the researchers noted that no subject experienced any discomfort during the experiment suggests that participants may not have experienced a phobic reaction. Morin and Garfinkle (1978) assessed behavioral correlates of homophobia. They used chair placement to determine the effect on social distance created by a person perceived as homosexual. Forty male and 40 female undergraduate participants were interviewed for ten minutes by either a male or a female experimenter who orally administered the Attitude Towards Homosexuality Scale. Increased social distance occurred when the experimenter was perceived to be homosexual and was of the same sex as the subject.

While this indicates avoidance behavior, which is a common feature of a phobic response, a phobic response involves multifactorial phenomena including cognitive-affective and behavioral domains. Without additional measures we cannot conclude that participants experienced a phobic response. It is possible that the observed avoidance was not mediated by fear or anxiety. Therefore, a tripartite approach to evaluating homophobia appears prudent, which involves cognitive, affective, and behavioral assessments (e.g., Herek & Berrill, 1990; Van de Ven, Bornholt & Bailey, 1996).

In the studies previously discussed, one or two aspects of the homophobic response were assessed. A more comprehensive approach to measurement is needed to aid understanding of homophobia. Knowledge about the nature of homophobia and its relationship to the phobic disorders is limited given that most research assessing homophobia, to date, has concentrated on paper and pencil assessment. Furthermore, many scales developed in the 1970s to measure homophobia, incorporated items, which measure a broad range of antihomosexual responses (i.e., homonegativism), rather than homophobia exclusively.

Another reason for assessing cognitive, affective, and behavioral domains involves the inconsistency sometimes found between cognition and behavior/affective state. For example, while Smith (1993) reported neutral to mildly positive scores for heterosexual respondents on the Attitudes Towards Gays and Lesbians Scale (ATGLS) (a measure of cognitive responses), homophobic scores on the IHP (which is argued to measure the affective domain) were identified for the same sample.

Clearly, the few empirical studies, which have examined the relationship between homophobia and the phobic disorders, have not provided conclusive findings. More research assessing the physiological and behavioral responses of individuals who score high and low on measures such as the IHP is clearly warranted. Certainly, heart rate and blood pressure measures taken while exposed to homosexual stimuli are two physiological measures of affective state which could help clarify the nature of homophobia and its relationship to other phobias, particularly when verbal analogue scales assessing fear, anger, and sexual arousal are concurrently taken. Given that these assessments are commonly used when investigating the nature of other phobic disorders and are relatively simple to employ, the paucity of such studies conducted to date is surprising.

There are a number of important reasons why research exploring the nature of homophobia should be undertaken. First, a number of researchers have questioned the appropriateness of using this term when describing all antihomosexual responses (e.g., Herek, 1984). In particular, it has been suggested that the label incorrectly psychologizes the concept of prejudice against gay males and lesbians (Herek, 1984; Herek, 1986). This view suggests that antihomosexual attitudes are underpinned by prejudice rather than fear. If this assertion is correct, clinical terms like diagnosis and treatment are not warranted. Unfortunately, at the moment, this view remains speculative as no conclusive data exist concerning the relationship between homophobia, fear, and prejudice.

Additionally, the perception of the behaviors and beliefs of homophobic individuals may be influenced by an increased understanding of the nature of homophobia. This would have broad social implications. Logan, for example, suggests that the "use of homophobia as a descriptor for anti-homosexual responses may be seen by society as implicit permission to continue the oppression of homosexuals, excused by its being the result of inescapable fear" (1996, p. 32). A common (and often successful) defense in criminal cases involving men who have murdered homosexuals is the assertion that being propositioned by a homosexual caused them to panic and react with force (Cunneen, Fraser, & Tomsen, 1997). The legitimacy of using a panic defense in this context could be clarified by research assessing the relationship between fear and homophobia. If no evidence is found for the proposition that homophobia is a valid clinical disorder, then such a defense would be illegitimate. Therefore, research examining the nature of homophobia is clearly warranted.

Negative attitudes and behavior toward homosexuals appears to be common. For example, a number of studies have found high levels in health care workers (Sullivan, 1996; Sullivan & Waite, 1997). One would expect this to potentially impact on the level of care given to clients perceived to be homosexual. In one study which utilized self report assessment on the modified version of the Index of Homophobia Scale (IHS) (Hudson & Ricketts, 1980), the majority of 165 psychiatric nurses indicated either moderate homophobia (57%) or severe homophobia (20%) (Smith, 1993).

IMPLICATIONS FOR INTERVENTIONS

While negative attitudes and behaviors towards homosexuals are common, they are not well understood. Antigay hate crimes (words or actions that are intended to harm or intimidate individuals because they are lesbian or gay) constitute a serious problem in many societies (e.g.,

Cunneen et al., 1997; Herek, 1989). In order to develop effective interventions, further research investigating the nature and prevalence of this phenomenon needs to be conducted (e.g., Van de Ven, 1995b; Van de Ven et al., 1996), particularly to delineate between the true homophobic subtype (hereinafter referred to as "true homophobia"), and prejudice (hereinafter referred to as "homoprejudice").

It has already been suggested that individuals who exhibit a true homophobic pattern of responding may require desensitization to overcome their fear (Shields & Harriman, 1984). The main treatment for phobic conditions includes behavior therapy techniques such as exposure and desensitization. The basis of this treatment involves progressively exposing clients to the object or situation they fear until their anxiety decreases (Andrews et al., 1994). However, educating clients so they can realistically assess their feared stimulus by disconfirming their excessive danger expectancies may also play a role in treatment. For example a client who has an intense fear of flying may be provided with information about the large number of passengers who use air travel every day and the extremely small number of deaths related to this form of travel over time.

However, if antihomosexual responses are more prejudice than fear based, it is suggested that interventions with a more focused role on education could be utilized in the reduction of antihomosexual responses (e.g., Ben-Ari, 1998; Herek, 1984; Serdahely & Ziemba, 1984; Uribe & Harbeck, 1992; Van de Ven, 1995b). According to Herek (1984), educational strategies may have a role in decreasing negative attitudes to homosexuals. These include sex education and the provision of accurate information to destroy myths and stereotypes held by homoprejudiced individuals. As noted by Van de Ven (1995b), the Department of School Education in the state of New South Wales, Australia, has recognized the importance of educational interventions aimed at decreasing antihomosexual prejudice. A teaching kit entitled *Resources for Teaching Against Violence* (New South Wales Department of School Education, 1991) has been designed for use by teachers and students in Years 9 to 12 in government schools. While there is a paucity of research investigating the effectiveness of educational interventions in reducing negative attitudes towards homosexuals, there are some published studies that have examined this issue.

Uribe and Harbeck (1992) reported that negative attitudes and stereotypes toward homosexuals and bisexuals can be altered using school-based educational programs. Using self-report measures they found an increased understanding and tolerance of homosexuality in over 300

American high school students after they had received information about homosexuality and bisexuality in health classes and watched a movie which showed a sympathetic portrayal of a gay high school student. Serdahely and Ziemba (1984) also found some evidence for the notion that education can reduce negative attitudes towards homosexuality. Forty-one students (26 female) completed a sexuality education unit that included readings, role-plays and discussions focusing on homosexuality. The control group consisted of 47 students (29 females and 25 males) who completed a drug education unit that contained no instruction on homosexuality. Students completed a modified version of the Hudson/Ricketts Index of Homophobia before and after they had completed their respective units. It was found that there was an overall reduction in scores on this measure of homonegativism only for students who received the homosexuality unit. The difference in scores for students in the homosexuality group who had pretest scores above the median when compared to the scores of control group counterparts was found to be statistically significant.

More recently, Ben-Ari (1998) also assessed the role of education in attitude change. He examined attitudes towards homosexuality of 46 social work students before and after an academic course, which involved 12 classes about individual, familial, and social aspects of homosexuality. He compared these measurements with those of 56 social work students who did not enroll in the course. It was found that the majority of students who had received the education unit significantly changed their attitudes towards homosexuality. Additionally, qualitative analyses indicated that these students had a more positive outlook and an increased awareness of the discriminatory nature of negative attitudes towards homosexuals.

Finally, Van de Ven (1995b) investigated the effectiveness of two teaching modules for reducing homonegativism in young offenders. Twenty-one young offenders participated in one teaching module and 16 in an alternative module. Both modules consisted of six sessions and entailed approximately five hours of instructional time (see further Van de Ven, 1995b for module details). Van de Ven concluded that while the attitude changes were only small in size, further development and evaluation of educational interventions with adolescents who hold negative attitudes towards homosexuals could prove fruitful.

While it has been suggested that stereotypes and prejudices are extremely resistant to change and such endeavors constitute "one of the most difficult in any undertaking of education in general and moral education in particular" (Aspin, 1999, p. 139), the findings from several studies have indicated that attitude change is possible. Future research may increase our understanding of how to reduce antihomosexual behavior by clarifying the utility of different intervention strategies, such as education and desensitization. As noted by Uribe and Harbeck (1992, p. 18), "experimental studies on intervention techniques and attitude development are important research problems for the future."

REFERENCES

Adams, H. E., Wright, L. W., & Lohr, B. A. (1996). Is homophobia associated with homosexual arousal? *Journal of Abnormal Psychology, 105*, 440-445.

American Psychiatric Association. (1980). *Diagnostic and statistical manual of mental disorders* (3rd ed.). Washington, DC: Author.

American Psychiatric Association. (1994). *Diagnostic and statistical manual of mental disorders: DSM-IV* (4th ed.) Washington, DC: Author.

Andrews, G., Crino, R., Hunt, C., Lampe, L., & Page, A. (1994). *The treatment of anxiety disorders*. Cambridge: Cambridge University Press.

Aspin, D. N. (1999). The nature of values and their place and promotion in schemes of values education. *Educational Philosophy and Theory, 31*, 123-143.

Bayer, R. (1981). *Homosexuality and American psychiatry: The politics of diagnosis*. New York: Basic Books.

Ben-Ari, A. T. (1998). An experiential attitude change: Social work students and homosexuality. *Journal of Homosexuality, 36*, 59-72.

Bhugra, D. (1987). Homophobia: A review of the literature. *Sexual and Marital Therapy, 2*, 169-177.

Council on Scientific Affairs. (1987). Aversion therapy. *Journal of the American Medical Association, 258*, 2562-2566.

Cunneen, C., Fraser, D., & Tomsen, S. (1997). *Faces of hate: Hate crime in Australia*. Sydney: Federation Press.

Herek, G. M. (1984). Beyond "homophobia": A social psychological perspective on attitudes toward lesbians and gay men. *Journal of Homosexuality, 10*, 1-21.

Herek. G. (1986). The social psychology of homophobia toward a practical theory. *Review of Law and Social Change, 14*, 923-934.

Herek, G. M. (1989). Hate crimes against lesbians and gay men: Issues for research and policy. *American Psychologist, 44*, 948-955.

Herek, G. M., & Berrill, K. T. (1990). Anti-gay violence and mental health: Setting an agenda for research. *Journal of Interpersonal Violence, 5*, 414-423.

Hudson, W. W., & Ricketts, W. A. (1980). A strategy for the measurement of homophobia. *Journal of Homosexuality, 5*, 357-372.

Kaplan, H., & Sadock, B. (1988). *Synopsis of Psychiatry*. (5th ed.). Baltimore: Williams and Wilkins.

Logan, C. R. (1996). Homophobia? No, homoprejudice. *Journal of Homosexuality, 31*, 31-53.

Morin, S. F., & Garfinkle, E. M. (1978). Male homophobia. *Journal of Social Issues, 34*, 29-47.

New South Wales Department of School Education. (1991). *Resources for teaching against violence.* Sydney, Australia: Author.

Ost, L.G., Sterner, U.L, & Lindahl, I.L. (1984). Physiological responses in blood phobics. *Behavior, Research & Therapy, 22*, 109-117.

Serdahely, W., & Ziemba, G. (1984). Changing homophobic attitudes through college sexuality education. *Journal of Homosexuality, 10*, 109-116.

Shields, S. A., & Harriman, R. E. (1984). Fear of male homosexuality: Cardiac responses of low and high homonegative males. *Journal of Homosexuality, 10*, 53-67.

Smith, G. B. (1993). Homophobia and attitudes toward gay men and lesbians by psychiatric nurses. *Archives of Psychiatric Nursing, 7*, 377-384.

Sullivan, G. (1987). *A study of political campaigns of discrimination against gay people in the United States, 1950-1978.* Ann Arbor, Michigan: University Microfilms International #8729425.

Sullivan, G. (1996). Health care services and the treatment of gay men and lesbians. In P. Martin (Ed.), *Back to the Future: A report from the third national Australian gay educators' conference.* (pp. 84-86). Sydney: Australian Federation of AIDS Organizations.

Sullivan, G. (2000). Donald Webster Cory. In R. Aldrich & G. Wotherspoon (Eds.), *Who's who in gay and lesbian history.* London: Routledge.

Sullivan, G., & Waite, H. (1997). Fact or fantasy: Educating health professionals about lesbian and gay clients. In J. Richters, R. Duffin, J. Gilmour, J. Irwin, R. Roberts, & A. Smith (Eds.). *Health in difference: Proceedings of the first national lesbian, gay, transgender and bisexual health conference.* Sydney: Australian Centre for Lesbian and Gay Research, University of Sydney.

Sykes, J.B. (Ed.). (1976). *The concise Oxford dictionary of current English.* Oxford University Press: London.

Uribe, V., & Harbeck, K. M. (1992). Addressing the needs of lesbian, gay, and bisexual youth: The origins of PROJECT 10 and school-based intervention. *Journal of Homosexuality, 22*, 9-28.

Van de Ven, P., Bornholt, L., & Bailey, M. (1996). Measuring cognitive, affective, and behavioral components of homophobic reaction. *Archives of Sexual Behavior, 25*, 155-179.

Van de Ven, P. (1994). Comparisons among homophobic reactions of undergraduates, high school students, and young offenders. *Journal of Sex Research, 31*, 117-124.

Van de Ven, P. (1995a). Talking with juvenile offenders about gay males and lesbians: Implications for combating homophobia. *Adolescence, 30*, 19-42.

Van de Ven, P. (1995b). A comparison of two teaching modules for reducing homophobia in young offenders. *Journal of Applied Social Psychology, 25*, 632-649.

Weinberg, G. (1972). *Society and the healthy homosexual.* New York: St. Martin's Press.

Wilbur, C. B. (1965). Clinical aspects of female homosexuality. In J. Marmor (Ed.), *Sexual inversion: The multiple roots of homosexuality* (pp. 268-281). New York: Basic Books.

Index

